You are God's signature. In *Your Signature Work,* Dianna Booher details how to make sure your signature stands for who you are—and are really meant to be.

LAURIE BETH JONES, founder and president of The Jones Group and author of *The Path: Creating Your Mission Statement for Work and for Life*

I have known Dianna Booher for fifteen years as a neighbor, fellow church member, and insightful author. She is a skilled communicator and an innovative consultant. *Your Signature Work* challenges readers to be their best and do their best. Translate that into reality as people practice the principles in this book, and you have star performers contributing to effective and efficient workplaces. I commend this book to everyone.

JIMMY DRAPER, president of LifeWay Christian Resources and author of *We Believe*

YOUR
SIGNATURE WORK

Creating Excellence
and Influencing Others at Work

Dianna Booher

TYNDALE HOUSE PUBLISHERS, INC.
WHEATON, ILLINOIS

Visit Tyndale's exciting Web site at www.tyndale.com

Your Signature Work: Pursuing God's Best at Work

Copyright © 2004 by Dianna Booher. All rights reserved.

Your Signature Life, Your Signature Work, and *Your Signature Self* are trademarks of Booher Consultants, Inc.

Cover photograph copyright © by Dynamic Graphics. All rights reserved.

Interior photographs on part openers one, two, four and six copyright © by Alamy. All rights reserved.

Interior photograph on part opener three copyright © by Photodisc. All rights reserved

Interior photograph on part opener five copyright © by PictureQuest LLC. All rights reserved.

Designed by Beth Sparkman

Edited by Susan Taylor

Published in association with the literary agency of Alive Communications, Inc., 7680 Goddard Street, Suite 200, Colorado Springs, CO 80920.

Unless otherwise indicated, all Scripture quotations are taken from the *Holy Bible,* New International Version®. NIV®. Copyright © 1973, 1978, 1984 by International Bible Society. Used by permission of Zondervan Publishing House. All rights reserved.

Scripture quotations marked "NKJV" are taken from the New King James Version. Copyright © 1979, 1980, 1982 by Thomas Nelson, Inc. Used by permission. All rights reserved.

Scripture quotations marked NASB are taken from the *New American Standard Bible,* © 1960, 1962, 1963, 1968, 1971, 1972, 1973, 1975, 1977 by The Lockman Foundation. Used by permission.

Scripture quotations marked NLT are taken from the *Holy Bible,* New Living Translation, copyright © 1996. Used by permission of Tyndale House Publishers, Inc., Wheaton, Illinois 60189. All rights reserved.

Scriptures marked CEV are taken from the Contemporary English Version © 1995 by American Bible Society. Used by permission.

Scriptures marked *The Message* are taken from *The Message.* Copyright © 1993, 1994, 1995, 1996, 2000, 2001, 2002. Used by permission of NavPress Publishing Group.

Library of Congress Cataloging-in-Publication Data

Booher, Dianna Daniels.
   Your signature work : pursuing God's best at work / Dianna Booher.
    p. cm.
   Includes bibliographical references.
   ISBN 0-8423-8281-X
   1. Employees—Religious life. 2. Work—Religious aspects—Christianity. I. Title.
   BV4593.B66 2004
   248.8'8—dc22   2004006376

Printed in the United States of America

10 09 08 07 06 05 04
7   6   5   4   3   2   1

CONTENTS

ACKNOWLEDGMENTS

An extra special thanks to the following individuals for their insights and experiences as managers, directors, vice presidents, presidents, CEOs, business owners, and consultants to major corporations: Tim Alba, Don O'Neal, Karen Rinehart, Troy King, Steve Drake, Jim Rhode, Ted McIllvain, Trisha Ragsdale, Kathy Hardcastle, Paul Rinehart, Jana Irwin, Yvette Franco, Todd Szalkowski, Karen Drake, Bill Hough, Don Hardcastle, Doug Slusher, Richard Luttrell, Allen Bechtel, Mike Duffy, Ken Harbin, and Mac Irwin.

They, as well as others whose names do not appear here, have provided invaluable observations and principles that have served them well in selecting, training, motivating, leading, evaluating, and rewarding all-star teams in the workplace.

Thanks to Kevin McGown for answering sports questions and also to Kevin Casey, a walking sports encyclopedia who was only a phone call away, for help with a sports statistic.

Jeff Booher and Vernon Rae read the manuscript to offer editorial suggestions.

Polly Fuhrman provided very capable assistance with research and final manuscript preparation.

Heartfelt thanks also to my editors at Tyndale, Tammy Faxel, Carol Traver, and Sue Taylor, for embracing the concept immediately and allowing me complete freedom to "run with it."

Any remaining fouls are my own. No basket.

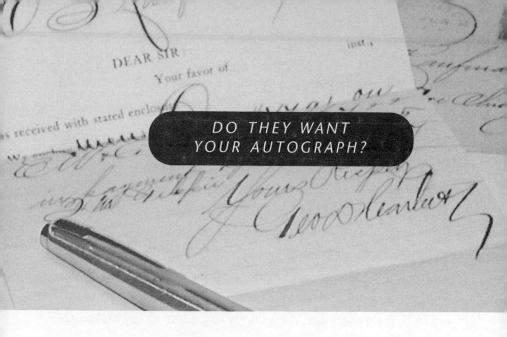

In our society, a signature sends a signal. It's a sign of commitment, authority, ownership, and recognition. We sign documents for a marriage license, a driver's license, or a home loan because we're making a *commitment* to love a person, follow the laws of the country, or repay a debt. We sign documents to give people *authority* to act on our behalf—withdraw money from our bank account or sell our house for us. We sign a document to take *ownership* for everything from a new car to a collie.

Those who create masterpieces, such as novels, movie scripts, songs, or sculptures, sign their names to their work. And those artists sign autographs for fans who recognize their accomplishments. Sports stars earn big bucks for their signature of endorsement on product lines. Because people *recognize* them as peak performers, the world takes notice of their opinions, values, and lifestyles. Their competence creates a *platform*.

What if a signature meant all these same things—commitment, authority, ownership, recognition for accomplishment, and a platform—in your job: committing to doing your personal best; taking authority and responsibility for results; working with such competence, manner, and mind-set that others were influenced positively by your message, values, and lifestyle.

Your Signature Work aims to help you do just that. My book *Your Signature Life* focuses on doing your personal best in three areas of life: building your character, your relationships, and your work. Just as artists sign their work when they finish, in effect saying, "This is my personal best," we sign our characters, marriages, friendships, and work every day. And God will be the final appraiser of the value we create.

In *Your Signature Life,* the analogy of building a dream house conveys the idea of doing our best at work. The Bible gives work great emphasis in our lives—as a blessing rather than a curse. Each of us has a calling in life and the power tools to build our masterpiece. Even if you feel trapped in a less-than-challenging job or career and think you don't count on God's radar screen, your work has significance. The attitude with which you serve makes all the difference. When you find that calling, your work produces great satisfaction and fulfillment—so much so, that it's difficult to discern what's work and what's play.

When others are attracted to your workplace personality and performance, you generate referrals for your faith and gain opportunities to exercise leadership on a larger scale. People want to follow a leader at work in the same way sports fans want to root for a winning ball team. Likewise, if your work style looks distinctive and your attitude attracts others rather than repels them, people will ask why and how questions of you. You will earn the right to be heard about your goals, values, beliefs, and faith. Your influence will spread. On the other hand, when you fail to work with integrity and your peers consider you a slacker, your influence suffers.

This new book, *Your Signature Work,* expands the concept of doing your personal best at work—paid or volunteer—by highlighting attitudes, traits, and skills that the Bible says make you a star performer. I've drawn parallels between the sport of basketball and the workplace to identify key principles of leadership, success, integrity, influence, and satisfaction. (Don't worry if you're not a basketball enthusiast. I haven't gone so deep into the sport that you'll miss the point of each chapter if you know nothing about basketball.)

Part 1: Show Up challenges you to get in the game emotionally with the right attitude rather than remain a spectator.

Part 2: Own Up focuses on the importance of accepting accountability for results.

Part 3: Follow Through addresses the typical problems of execution—how to get the ball to the basket and actually through the hoop.

Part 4: Keep Your Focus provides help with the intangibles that tend to overwhelm us in complex work situations such as tough decisions, problem solving, timing, and simplifying tasks.

Part 5: Run, Play Hurt, or Sit Out—but Don't Whine explores the value of creating a positive reputation and a positive culture, along with insight on resolving conflict.

Part 6: Sign On for Life suggests what to do if your work conflicts with your personal relationships and your commitments to God and how to use your "off-season" appropriately to be a well-rounded person.

Evidence in the workplace bears out these same principles of productivity, praise, and profit. For the past twenty-four years as a consultant to major corporations, I've dealt with employees at all levels—general professionals, middle and senior managers, and top executives. During these client interactions, I've observed star performers who deliver results, staff problems that stall organizations, executives' reasons for hiring, career-development decisions, and termination decisions. Additionally, I've interviewed successful managers and executives specifically for this book to gather their observations about what distinguishes star performers from other employees.

So get your head in the game, and consider the following strategies and plays as you perform Your Signature Work.

PART ONE

SHOW UP

*P*laywright Woody Allen first uttered this now famous line: "Eighty percent of success is showing up." A few people fail to show up in life—for their kids, for their friends, for their own best interests. Even more people fail to show up at work—emotionally, that is—and if they show up, they don't suit up.

Some players act as though they'd just as soon stay in the locker room as play on the court. They show up for practice late, and they're the first ones to hit the showers afterward. They stay out late and eat the wrong foods before the big games. During important tournaments they're focused on who's in the stands, how sore their muscles are, how tired they are, how the opponent looked on the way out of the locker room, what the coach said to the referee—everything but winning.

If the coach doesn't call their name in the starting lineup, they shrug and take a seat on the bench with a sigh of relief. They don't have to remember plays, study the opponents, change strategy, or pay attention to the score.

Star performers, however, suit up and show up to play. They demonstrate flexibility, accept new ideas, embrace change, and take initiative. They've made an emotional investment in winning the game.

ONE

SIGN UP FOR THE SEASON

Sports arenas seat two kinds of fans: those who show up *now and then* to have a good time with friends and those who show up at *every* game because they're committed to the team for the long haul. Generally, this second group has an emotional attachment. They are exuberant when the team wins and deflated when the team loses.

In fact, we can divide this second group, the season-ticket holders, into two camps. One group buys tickets when they expect a winning season—for example, when their team has a top draft choice who's the talk of the media. The second group of season-ticket holders buys tickets year after year for decades. They're a loyal lot. They plan their vacations, family reunions, and even weddings around the team's schedule. You may know some of these fans or be one yourself.

Like these fans, Signature Stars show up season after season, no matter what. They're in the game long term and make an emotional investment in the organizations that employ them. They suit up to play and take on whatever challenges come their way.

Have you ever been to a party and engaged in a conversation with someone who's continually glancing over your shoulder during the conversation? You get the feeling that when someone more interesting comes along, that person is going to bolt from the conversation.

Bosses and teammates have the same feeling with team members who work as though they've suited up for just one game or tournament. They become disappointed in peers who seem uninterested in the reasons behind decisions, the market for their products or services, the financial picture, or the industry players and predicaments. And understandably, they hesitate to devote time to bring such people up to speed because they're unsure how long those employees will be around and what the payoff will be for their efforts.

> *If you aren't fired with enthusiasm, you will be fired*
> *with enthusiasm.*   —VINCE LOMBARDI

I've made my share of mistakes in selecting applicants who weren't excited about getting in the game, hiring them just because we needed five people on the court. A woman with a master's degree in English applied for a job as editor of our training materials, which was a perfect fit on paper. On the day she was to report for work three weeks later, she phoned to say she'd moved across the country to write a novel. Then there was the consultant we hired who couldn't learn her new job because she was always talking about how "back at the old job, the way we always did it was to X. Are you sure your approach here really works?"

Several years ago our new chief operating officer spent his

first half-year unexpectedly flying across the country back to his old employer, trying to put out fires and wind down projects because "they needed help" and he was "the only one who knew what was going on." The praise of a few colleagues at the old place made it difficult to pull up roots and start over to rebuild that sense of accomplishment in his new position.

None of these players had yet made the emotional switch to their new team. In the case of the novelist, we were fortunate to discover her lack of commitment before we had made any investment in salary or training. With the latter two, the discovery cost us a great deal of time, money, and lost opportunity in finding a more invested player sooner.

> *Enthusiasm is contagious—and so is the lack of it.*
>
> —UNKNOWN

Sometimes it's those at the very top of the food chain who don't show up or suit up to play. In their best-selling book *Execution: The Discipline of Getting Things Done,* Larry Bossidy, chairman of Honeywell International, and Ram Charan, insist on the critical importance of leaders showing up for their employees—rather than remaining detached, removed, and absent. Some senior executives don't care enough about the day-to-day operations to show up to talk with the people running their various divisions. Leaders show up to quiz their stars about their numbers, to ask them about their challenges, to give them a performance review, and to discuss their career goals.

If you are a leader, you don't need charisma. You just need to invest emotionally in the people who work for you and with you. You need to care that they personally succeed.

The same is true at any level in any group. Coworkers expect you to commit for a season—wholeheartedly, not just until someone comes along and offers a few dollars more in salary, a better sounding title, or a bigger office with a better view. Before you can expect bosses to invest time to give you special training, plum assignments, and high-visibility projects, you have to demonstrate that you're going to stay for a season— or better yet, several seasons.

To become a basketball celebrity, it takes more than one game; it takes a season or several seasons. And to become a star at work, it takes more than just showing up physically. You have to show up emotionally. The Bible says, "Whatever you do, do well."[1] Are you committed enough to tell your family and friends to buy season tickets?

*D*o you "show up" on every project you lead? Do you "show up" every day that you take home a paycheck?

The road to failure is greased with the slime of indifference.

—UNKNOWN

✳ **As a Signature Star, Your Autograph Says You . . .**
Make an emotional investment in your organization and in the people around you.

TWO

FOCUS ON OFFENSE, NOT DEFENSE

Both defense and offense win ball games. But winning teams focus on running plays that get the ball to their small forward, power forward, and center to put points on the board. Of course, they have to play defensively to block an opponent's shots, rebound, and steal the ball. But if they concentrate *only* on defense, they'll likely lose.

Some employees adopt a similarly limiting strategy in the workplace. Their disposition is defense. They guard against accepting anything new—new structure, new procedures, new responsibilities, new policies, new people, new ideas.

Have you ever attended a meeting where the big kahuna from each department can't attend but sends a representative instead? If you have, then you've probably seen this phenomenon unfold. These representatives generally show up with one agenda from their boss: "Attend the meeting, and don't let X happen. Protect our turf." In other words, they don't have enough understanding of the issue or enough authority to offer creative solutions. All their boss expects is that they refuse to go along with any decisions at the meeting until the absent boss has an opportunity to review the ideas and cast a vote. So they guard the status quo. They play defense to prevent others' action plans from passing. Corporations are bursting at the seams with such defensive posturing and stubbornness.

Doug Slusher, area supervisor for a national petroleum company, ran into resistance when senior management decided to install new register systems throughout their chain of retail service stations across the country. Three managers in his area decided to play defensively and not train their store employees to run the new computers and registers. As a result, they all lost their jobs because their stores could no longer grow.

> *Keep changing. When you're through changing,*
> *you're through.*   —BRUCE BARTON

After ten years as a star performer, Yvette Franco was promoted to a new position as director of brand and product development for a large cosmetics company. She assumed leadership of a technical group that was expecting a top-notch color expert to take the helm. But executive management had promoted her to the new position because of her leadership skills, not necessarily for her technical expertise. As soon as she assumed the new position, it became clear which members of her team intended to focus on offense and which intended to focus on defense. In the eight months since she has taken over leadership of the department, she has seen the power forwards distinguish themselves and excel in their assignments. Those playing defensively have fallen further and further behind.

This kind of resistance happens often after a merger or the placement of new management. Many people leave; some people stay. Others stay physically but leave mentally. When Signature Stars stay, they focus on scoring.

Others adopt a defensive strategy and resist change for any number of reasons: (1) They're comfortable with the status quo. (2) They don't understand the reason for the change and can't grasp the vision for how things will be after a change. They aren't sold on the idea that different will necessarily be better, so why take a chance? (3) Their track record with change has been failure after failure. If past attempts at changes have generated criticism and ended in false starts, they'll not be eager to try, try again. (4) They may not like the person leading the change. (5) Peer pressure may hold them in check. If their best friends play defensively, they may not want to be the only player focusing on offense.

These reasons are understandable. They just don't necessarily win games or produce rewards or results at work.

> *Everybody is in favor of progress. It's the change they don't like.* —UNKNOWN

A senior executive for a large pharmaceutical company recalls the resistance he ran into several years ago from a group of employees when his organization began to implement the standards of the ISO.[1] One of his star performers, Mary Lou, came to him concerned that the rest of the group was not ready to meet the challenge on the new court. Her attitude was to play ball: "Okay, what do we need to do to get everybody with us?"

She offered the executive, Troy, a proposal: She wanted to

write a skit and dress up like Troy to address these ISO issues in the skit. She felt that she could mimic him in a lighthearted way (Troy's a large man), say things in fun that employees would never say or ask in a straightforward manner, and break down her colleagues' resistance to change with humor. Troy gave her the go-ahead and set up three employee assemblies of four hundred employee groups for her "performance." It worked. The employees loved it, dropped the defensive strategy, and began to concentrate on the offense to learn the new standards.

Everyone needs power forwards like Mary Lou on their team.

Jesus Christ himself focused on moving forward rather than defending the status quo. He began his ministry to change the way the religious community did things. He turned their strict interpretations of hundreds of religious laws upside down to set people free to live by two commandments: Love the Lord God with all your heart, soul, and mind, and love others as yourself.[2] He changed the way they worshiped and the focus of their teaching to include people of all races. Their worship often took place in their homes as well as in synagogues. Women as well as men joined in their praise, ministry, and spread of the gospel.

He changed their social world, elevating both women and children in their society and selecting those from the most common occupations as spiritual leaders to carry out his mission. In fact, there's not much he didn't change during his brief work on earth.

Signature Stars embrace change. When they meet challenges and problems, they lean forward toward the goal. They concentrate on offensive scoring, not their blocks and steals. Rather than defend and guard the status quo, they focus on stream-

lining a process, improving service, repositioning people for
better use of their talents, and improving overall profitability.

*I*n your workplace, are you known for adding points to the
score or just holding others back? When new ideas surface,
are you a revolutionary or a reactionary?

New ideas hurt some minds the same as new shoes
hurt some feet.   —UNKNOWN

✳ **As a Signature Star, Your Autograph Says You . . .**
Embrace change and new ideas.

THREE

SUIT UP

"Get your head in the game!" "Watch the ball!" "Pay attention to your passes!" Let the lethargy go on too long, and the player will be on the bench. Being benched in the sports world is a bad thing; your stats suffer. Sit there too long and your career is shot.

But at work, far too many people are happy to sit on the bench. They prefer a spot as spectator rather than initiator of anything but the assigned tasks.

Initiative becomes natural only when curiosity and learning meet passion.

Jack Welch, former CEO of General Electric, also understood the importance of initiative from the days he was just an engineer running tests. In his autobiography, *Jack: Straight from the Gut,* he tells about his mind-set at the beginning of his climb up the corporate ladder. Speaking of his boss and a big promotion that opened a key door for him, he says:

> We had met in several business reviews. We had made a connection because I would always give him more than he

expected. As a junior development engineer, I had given him a complete cost and physical property analysis of our new plastic versus every major competing product offered by the DuPonts, Dows, and Celaneses of the world. It projected the long-range product costs of nylong, polypropylene, acrylic, and acetel against our products.

It was by no means an earth-shattering analysis, but was more than the usual from a guy in a white lab coat.

What I was trying to do was "get out of the pile." If I had just answered his questions, it would have been tough to get noticed. Bosses usually have answers in mind when they hand out questions. They're just looking for confirmation. To set myself apart from the crowd, I thought I had to think bigger than the questions posed. I wanted to provide not only the answer, but an unexpected fresh perspective.[1]

Promotions have their genesis in such efforts—even though those who take initiative in their jobs do so out of habit. It's just the way they play every game they suit up for.

LEARNING GETS PEOPLE OFF THE BENCH

My friend Danny Cox, coauthor of *Leadership When the Heat's On*, says, "To achieve great things, know more than the average person considers necessary."[2]

I remember early in my career talking with the secretary to a senior vice president of an oil company. As we chatted in the lobby, I asked her to tell me what she enjoyed most about her job. "Little lessons," was her instant reply. She then explained that executives from her own organization, suppliers, customers, and foreign dignitaries were in and out of her office weekly. She overheard many of the discussions that unfolded in the nearby conference room. She acted as her boss's representative in transactions with foreign dignitaries, handled most of his personal financial affairs, and represented him internally during his long absences due to international travel.

"Often, in the heat of discussions, decisions, and crises, there's no time to explain the reasoning of all the players. But I wait until things settle down. Then I call up another vice president or snag my boss for a moment and say, 'Hey, I need a little lesson about what happened the other day.' And I ask questions. About the background. The analysis. The pros and cons of a decision. I just love learning about new areas of the company, the industry, how people think. And people love explaining things."

Later I discovered that this very effective administrative assistant drew an almost six-figure salary—in the mid-1980s. Those who take initiative contribute value and are often rewarded handsomely.

The director of operation services at Alcon Laboratories talks fondly about one such employee, not an engineer but someone with previous training in lighting. The company was experiencing a huge problem in getting a particular drug to market because the lighting in their labs altered the temperature, which, of course, altered the drug. This particular lab employee took the initiative to do additional research on his own time. Gathering data from the space program, he figured out a way to measure intensity and exposure when competitors were unable to do so. His resulting work solved a very big problem for his organization.

Those who continually put forth effort to learn show initiative.

God holds us responsible, not for what we have, but what
we could have; not for what we are, but for what we
might be.   —UNKNOWN

CURIOSITY GETS PEOPLE OFF THE BENCH

Those who take initiative typically do so even when they're not
taking home a paycheck. A couple in the Dallas–Fort Worth area
took on the challenge of chairing a volunteer committee to market their child's parochial school to the community—without
spending money. After discovering that the school's single largest
fund-raiser each year was a dinner and auction, they decided to
break out of the rut and call other schools around the country to
find out what they'd done to make their fund-raisers successful.
As a result, they raised $118,000 for the elementary school in one
evening. And nobody had to tap them on the shoulder and say,
"Rather than preside over the past, why don't you investigate
how other schools meet this challenge?"

Mike Duffy, president of CTN (Corporate Television
Network), credits his secretary with taking the initiative to save
his organization thousands of dollars in cost-cutting measures.
In her spare moments she decided to check into their life insurance options and discovered that the company could increase
their coverage from $100,000 to $500,000 per employee for $10
less per month. Next she told the organization to stop paying
into her own retirement plan because she was sixty-one years
old and didn't intend to be working for the ten-year minimum
required to receive the payout. That saved them another $250
per month. Then she started slashing their stationery costs and
meetings costs. She understands that small savings make a big
impact on the total profit picture.

What's more, nobody told her to investigate any of these cost-cutting ideas. She took the initiative to do so herself. Curiosity can drive initiative.

PASSION GETS PEOPLE OFF THE BENCH

One organization, a national pizza chain, feels so strongly about its employees' taking initiative that if they aren't playing the court proactively, they not only get benched, they get dropped from the team. A senior executive explains it this way: "We want people to own a goal passionately. We give them incentives each quarter based on their goals. We expect them to initiate their own goals proactively. And if they don't, they're terminated—even if they do their job as assigned. It's part of our culture. They sign a Declaration of *Interdependence* between management and employees. I just had to let a guy go, a friend of mine, who has been here for four years. He does his job—but that's all. We expect more than that."

Initiative doesn't have to involve big analysis, big answers, big ideas. Little suggestions also serve well. Trisha Ragsdale, senior producer of a popular national television show, loves for her staffers to come to her with suggestions such as this: "I was watching another segment on NBC last week, and I noticed X. Can we do that?" Whether or not they make the change is irrelevant. The fact that they're watching other networks on their own time with an alert mind says volumes about their passion for their work.

Passion drives initiative. Without it, the adrenaline stops pumping. Players lose their edge.

Opponents aren't going to tap you on the shoulder and say, "You can steal the ball now—I'm about to throw a sloppy pass."

As a Signature Star, you take initiative to contribute ideas, save money, improve processes, raise standards, and create higher value for your customers. Initiative adds another dimension—excitement—to your story. It's the three-pointer from behind the arc that surprises and delights your fans.

When was the last time you jumped for a rebound or stole the ball and made a fast break for the basket?

If there is no wind, row.   —LATIN PROVERB

✷ **As a Signature Star, Your Autograph Says You . . .**
Take initiative.

FOUR

LEARN MORE THAN ONE PLAY

Have you ever watched a team that seemed to run one play over and over, regardless of the score and regardless of the opponent?

It may be a complex and beautiful play and one that's difficult to stop. But if a team runs it every time, the opposition soon catches on that the play isn't going to change. If the first team persists in trying to run the same play, they'll soon find themselves in trouble. The defenders stop following the decoys.

One play, no matter how great it works, won't get your team to the Olympics. That's why winning teams and star players know the importance of flexibility.

In the workplace where flexibility is called for, some people can't and others won't. Although it's up to leaders to decide which is the case in a given situation, neither of those responses looks good on an employee's official scoreboard.

Take, for example, the casualties supervisor in a large insurance agency in Houston who was demoted because he refused to be flexible about how he served his clients. He had once been successful in the business of handling his clients and staying in touch through paper—formal letters, hard-copy reports, printed forms. But clients began to ask for faster communication—by fax, then by e-mail. He couldn't run those plays. He got further and further behind in his responses and reports to the clients and management he served. Although he was brilliant, he remained inflexible about his procedures.

For a while he was a one-play superstar. But his fans expected him to play on different courts at different times of the day against different opponents. And he couldn't flex.

> *I can't understand why people are frightened of new ideas.*
> *I'm frightened of the old ones.*
>
> —JOHN CAGE, MUSICIAN AND COMPOSER

A survey of fifteen thousand employees nationwide conducted by Bavendam Research confirms that the majority of workers rank the opportunity to learn and broaden their skills among the top three benefits employers offer. In short, they demand a challenge and want opportunities to stretch their muscles and make themselves more flexible.[1]

For some people, however, inflexibility represents a mind-set, not a lack of skill. That was the case in a hospital system in the Philadelphia area during the midst of a computer system installation, for which all twelve hospitals and the president had signed off. Julia, the director in charge of five departments, revolted and walked out of a hospital-staff training program for the new system. Following her example, five department managers who report to her also bolted. Shortly thereafter, they all discovered that neither they nor their staff could get scheduled or paid until they learned how to use the new system.

Although they complained adamantly, they quickly learned
to run a new play.

The Bible offers two models of flexibility in working mode.

PAUL

The apostle Paul demonstrated great flexibility in his ministry:
"I have learned to be content whatever the circumstances."[2]
He seemed equally motivated to win the world, whether from
a jail cell or from the synagogue. He also showed flexibility in
his preaching style. To the educated, he appealed to intellect
and reasoning. To those of other races, he laced his sermons
with references to their culture.[3] To the uneducated masses,
he preached a simple, straightforward message.

JESUS

Christ himself was flexible. He did his work of preaching, teaching, and healing wherever necessary—on the hillside, in the
temple, on the street, in friends' homes. His methods also varied
from situation to situation. Sometimes he opened the Scriptures
and expounded on them formally in the synagogue. At other
times, he told the crowd a story to make a single point. Sometimes he used a dramatic situation and object lesson to drive
home a point at a teachable moment, such as the time a crowd
was ready to stone a woman caught in adultery. He bent down
and began to write in the sand; then he responded, "If any one
of you is without sin, let him be the first to throw a stone at
her."[4] At that, all the woman's accusers left the scene. On still
other occasions, Jesus did his work behind closed doors and let
others interpret his message to the masses.

Many followed him and began to spread his message in their

own way. At one point the disciples came to Jesus and said, "We saw a man driving out demons in your name and we told him to stop, because he was not one of us." In other words, they were saying, "There are people going about doing this or that, and it's not the way we do things. Should we stop them?" Jesus told the disciples to leave the man alone, saying, "Whoever is not against us is for us."[5]

That's an example of flexibility to the max.

As a Signature Star at work, you have to be able to dribble, pass, run, block, guard, rebound, and shoot. Developing only one skill set—or persisting in only one mind-set—will limit both your personal growth and your value to the organization.

*A*re you learning to run more than one play?

Many people hate any change that doesn't jingle in their pockets.   —UNKNOWN

★ **As a Signature Star, Your Autograph Says You . . .**
Demonstrate flexibility.

FIVE

PLAY WITH A WHOLE-COURT PERSPECTIVE

It's difficult to see who has the ball when you have a seven-foot player towering over you with two huge hands in your face. It's worse still when you're on your knees with the ball trapped on the floor, two teammates darting in and out waiting for you to pass off, with defenders waving arms to block any such attempts. The one thing you hate to hear from a fan in the stands at the next time-out? "Number 24 was completely open under the goal. Why didn't you throw it?"

Of course, it's often easier for spectators to see the whole court. They can choose to sit high in the stands. And obviously, the view from some seats is better than from others. That's why the club sells good seats, better seats, and the best seats and prices the tickets accordingly. Rather than being locked into one free-throw lane with a limited view, they can see all the action. But spectators aren't players. As an inexperienced player in the middle of the game, it's difficult to see the whole court, so it's tempting to keep an eye only on the opponent defending you and on a teammate or two nearby.

If you watch elementary age kids play ball, you'll see this myopia in action. As soon as players get the ball, they pass it off to the closest open teammate. But as experienced players make their way to the pros, they learn to make the effort to look at the entire court and know who's where.

You need the same vantage point in the workplace—the view from the stakeholder's perspective.

We mentioned Yvette Franco earlier. As vice president of brand and product development at a large cosmetics company, Yvette has a marketing manager who definitely understands the big picture beyond marketing: "Our business is about the sales force, and this particular manager shows that interest in a genuine way. Typically, when a marketing project is killed—for whatever reason—the manager of that project may mope for a month. But she doesn't. She gets over it and moves on. And what's more, she has her mind on the good of the company as a whole. For example, we're looking at a new compact idea. . . . She came up with a totally new approach on packaging. It fits the concept, and it has excited our whole company. Word immediately traveled after this meeting throughout the company. The president even called her. It will have a huge impact. So she has obviously been thinking outside of her job responsibilities."

Had this manager stayed focused on her small area of play— designing a marketing campaign for product X—would she ever have had this kind of impact? Probably not, no matter how well the product she was responsible for marketing might have sold.

Our government leaders have broadened their perspective in the last five decades to understand the impact of their decisions and actions, not only on the citizens of the United States but also on citizens of the entire free world. CEOs of large corporations, as well, understand that their decisions and actions affect not only their employees and the U.S. stock market but a global workforce and economy.

No matter whose payroll you're on or whether you sign the payroll checks, to have a huge impact you need a wider view of the court. Specifically, that means:

Spend your time where it counts. If you were paying someone else to do your job, how would you want that person to spend his time? That question will help you spot nonessential tasks and misdirected efforts. When you think like an owner, you're not focused on putting in your hours but on getting the job done—whatever hours it takes to do it right.

> *Competence, like truth, beauty and contact lenses, is in the eye of the beholder.* —LAURENCE J. PETER

Calculate your profit and loss on contributions made and value delivered. Think "Inc." If you haven't already incorporated in reality, think of yourself in that light. If you were a contractor going to work every day to sell your skills on the open market, what could you charge and what valuable service would you deliver? To think like an owner and have an owner's perspective, consider your value versus your cost. Literally, calculate your contribution minus your expense (salary, benefits, and portion of overhead) to your organization. Are you a good value for the money? If not, how could you upgrade the value you're adding?

Avoid territorialism and turf wars. When you think like an owner, you have little patience with pettiness: who told whom what first; who gets credit for an idea; who has seniority; who is left off the distribution list; whose budget gets lopped off first or last. Instead, your focus becomes what makes sense for the entire organization.

Put team interests above self-interests. Understand that all the history, facts, data, reasons, results, and intentions are not revealed in one isolated incident on the far side of the court. The owner has to investigate and analyze what's happening to all the players on the team and then make a decision based on all the data available and the anticipated payoff.

Granted, it's a lot tougher to see all the players when you're in the game rather than seated in the stands. But then, that's what makes a Signature Star.

*W*hen was the last time you passed the ball to someone open on the other side of the court and let them take the shot?

Change your thoughts and you change your world.

—NORMAN VINCENT PEALE

★ **As a Signature Star, Your Autograph Says You . . .**
See the big picture.

SIX

ARRIVE IN TIME FOR THE TIP-OFF

The excitement of the tip-off swells: toes to toes, knees to knees, elbows to elbows around the center circle. The two tallest players crouch, poised to spring into the air at the sound of the referee's whistle and the toss of the ball. Whoever leaps highest and tips the ball to one of her teammates at the opening whistle gives her team the advantage from the start.

How long do you think a college player would last on the first string if she continually arrived too late for the tip-off? What if this talented player habitually showed up well into the first quarter—or even after the warm-up drills had begun and before the players took the court for the opening play?

The coach might accept a plausible explanation on the first occasion and deliver a stern warning. On a subsequent late arrival, the player would likely be dropped from the starting lineup. If there were other such incidents, the player would most likely be dropped from the team. Punctuality is a big deal in the sports world.

But in the business world, some performers minimize its importance. They routinely show up to work ten to twenty minutes late each day. They show up to meetings late and keep everyone who must have their input or consensus waiting. They turn in reports or data a day late and delay others who are waiting for the information. They follow up client leads a week late—after buyers have given up and decided to buy from the competition.

Maybe they've never put a calculator to the hard or soft cost of punctuality fouls. Let's talk hard costs first.

LOSS OF PRODUCTIVITY

Let's say an employee who earns $50,000 a year is fifteen minutes late twice a week. That amounts to $1,300 a year. If the company has one thousand employees at that salary level and all of them are fifteen minutes late twice a week, those late starts cost the company $1.3 million a year in lost productivity.

Now think about the clock ticking away the minutes while someone does "just one more thing" before arriving. Let's say that same $50,000 employee arrives fifteen minutes late and keeps six other people (at the same salary level) waiting because they need his or her input or consensus. If they meet only once a week, it amounts to $3,900 in annual waiting time. Multiply that cost times the number of various team or group meetings during any given year to get an idea of the annual cost of keeping people waiting in meetings.

Now for the bigger costs.

LOSS OF OPPORTUNITY AND IMAGE

Many years ago, when I was just starting out in business and before the days of the prominent use of cell phones, I had only one employee, an office manager who was scheduled to work from nine to three each day. Before and after those hours, an answering service took our calls. Although Jan performed well in most areas, she failed to understand the importance of getting to work promptly at nine and generally arrived somewhere between nine ten and nine thirty. Because I typically worked at a client's site, I didn't know how often this happened until I began to receive comments like these from clients and prospects: "I phoned your office about nine fifteen and got an answering service. I had assumed your organization was a little larger and that you had a staff person. That gives me second thoughts about dealing with a company so small." Or, "Your office manager didn't answer when I called at nine o'clock this morning, so I wasn't able to get the information I needed for my budget meeting at nine thirty. My colleague came to our staff meeting with all the information on another consulting firm he wants to hire. So my boss made a decision to go with the other firm because we didn't have your information available at our meeting."

It's difficult to assign a dollar amount to lost opportunities like these. Nevertheless, lack of punctuality plays a part that employers can't recoup. It's part of the package for Signature Stars.

*D*o you always show up for the tip-off?

The drawback of being punctual is that there's nobody
to appreciate it.   —UNKNOWN

✳ As a Signature Star, Your Autograph Says You . . .
Meet deadlines and show up on time.

PART TWO

OWN UP

*I*n football a team gets four tries to make a first down. Baseball players get three strikes to get on base. Tennis players have two attempts to make a good serve. Volleyball players get three passes to place the ball over the net. Soccer players can scramble and kick as many times as possible to make a goal. Basketball players take as many shots as they can rebound to make a basket.

Final results, not first attempts, determine the overall score in most sports.

The same is true at work. While the list is short of people who take on additional responsibilities not assigned to them and that do not offer personal benefit, accountability for results wins respect.

SEVEN

PLAY YOUR POSITION

When your team loses, it's easy to place blame: The opposing team was taller, bigger, stronger, more experienced. Their coaching staff had a better track record. They had the top draft choice. The officials made too many bad calls. They had the home-court advantage. Your star player suffered an injury and left the game in the first quarter.

If those explanations aren't accepted, you can start on your own teammates: They didn't get open under the basket. They didn't rebound. They took too many low-percentage shots. The zone defense wasn't working. The guards fouled too often.

But when you're standing at the free-throw line all alone— no defenders blocking your view, no ticking clock to add pressure—and you miss the basket, you're fully accountable. There's no one else to blame.

Playing your position at work means being accountable for what happens and accepting responsibility for results—with no one else to blame. Individual accountability has been a struggle for us ever since Adam and Eve lived in the Garden of Eden:

"Who me?" Adam might have said. "I'm not responsible for keeping records about which trees are off limits. It was the woman, Eve, you gave me—she's the one who told me to eat the forbidden fruit. She sent up the paperwork; I just signed off on it. I don't have time to read everything that crosses my desk."

Then Eve took her turn, hedging: "Who me? I wasn't the final decision maker on this deal. Besides, we had a temp in the Garden that day. He was a real snake."

But the Bible clears up the accountability issue rather pointedly: "Each of us will have to give a personal account to God."[1]

Again, in the Gospels, the Parable of the Talents sets forth the idea that responsible people are accountable for what they've been given in life.[2] The master divides the talents among his servants according to their abilities and tells them to invest the money and manage it until he returns. The talents represent any resources someone receives—talents, skills, money, time, gifts, or wisdom. Two servants invest the money and are rewarded for their faithfulness. One does not, fearing to be accountable for results. The master returns and expresses great displeasure at this last servant, who refused to accept responsibility.

Many people in the workplace are like the third worker in this parable, burying their talent in the ground and refusing to play their position. They blame everybody and everything when things aren't going right on the job. Like a basketball player, they are standing at the free-throw line, shooting at the basket, missing right and left, and blaming someone else.

REASONING GONE AWRY

When employees reject responsibility, they reason backward. Their comments sound like these:

- I don't *have* $20,000 in my budget. Therefore, I *can't schedule* training for my staff. So there's *no way* we're going to *be* a quality team.
- I don't *have* a mentor. Therefore, I *can't get good feedback* on my performance. So I'll *never be* a great salesperson.
- I don't *have* talented people working for me. Therefore, we aren't going to *finish our projects* on time, within budget, to the quality standards specified in the contract. So I'll *never become* a leader with opportunities to influence my division in ethical matters.

These people have abdicated accountability in their lives. Notice that someone has "taken" something from them. Therefore, they can't "do" something, which limits their ability to "be" someone. A responsible person would flip all the previous situations and comments and reason as follows:

- We plan to *be* a quality team. Therefore, I need to *schedule* a training class for my staff. I need to find a way to *generate, save, or negotiate* for $20,000 in my budget.
- I want to *be* a great salesperson. Therefore, I'll need to *find a coach* so I can *get good feedback* on my performance.
- I want to *become* a leader with opportunities to influence my division in ethical matters. Therefore, I'll have to *earn respect from others with a team that finishes projects* on time, within budget, and meets quality standards. So I'm going to need to *recruit, hire, train, and retain* talented people to work for me.

Accountability is about holding the ball in your hands, looking at the positions of your teammates, glancing at the game clock, and deciding for yourself whether to pass, dribble, or shoot. It takes courage to call your own plays.

> *Those who shrink from responsibilities keep on shrinking*
> *in other ways too.*   —UNKNOWN

A director of operations talks about one of the highlights of his twenty-five-year career: "We needed to buy or lease a new facility for an acquisition we were about to make. It was bleeding about $3 to 4 million a month, and we needed to get the expenses under control. So that was in my realm of responsibility. My team studied the problem, and then I went to the president and said, 'I can fix the problem in about four months if you'll give us the money.'

"The president asked, 'How much?'

"'Two million.'

"'You got it,' he said, 'but you better deliver.'

"And we did. We looked like heroes. We took full accountability for our plan. We told him we'd use our experience from previous acquisitions to hire consultants and make all the related decisions. Sure enough, we stopped the financial blood flow in four months. This division is now our most profitable. But he would never have let us have the money if we had not accepted full responsibility for the results."

In the current work culture with teams driving almost every initiative, it's difficult to find an individual or department who accepts full responsibility for a situation. Rather, it's far too easy to shrug your shoulders and pass the ball of blame to the next team or individual on the list.

In recent years individuals have attempted to take responsibility for their personal development—character traits, attitude, and career development—with performance tools and peer feedback systems. Some have been successful in making significant changes in their personality and performance, based on how others perceive them. Others have shrugged off peers' perceptions as unwarranted and plunged ahead, persisting in old habits.

Accountability can be tough or rewarding, depending on your purpose and ego strength.

ARTICLES OF ACCOUNTABILITY

You may want to consider adopting the following *Articles of Accountability* as a way to paint a key on the court at your workplace and force yourself to stand behind the free-throw line on occasion, just as other people have to do.

Expect As Much from Yourself As You Do from Those above You

People in positions of authority are human beings struggling with the same weaknesses, worries, and warts that we all have. Why hold them to some superstandard that you yourself do not model and criticize them for infractions that you would not want to be criticized for? They fail just like everyone else. Continually complaining about what the "powers that be" or politicians or the government should do is pointless.

> *The thing I like about baseball is that it's one on one. You stand up there alone, and if you make a mistake, it's your mistake. If you hit a home run, it's your home run.*
>
> —HANK AARON

Commit to the Success of Your Organization

Why should your organization have to earn your loyalty? Did your parents have to earn your love? Did your school have to earn your respect? Does your favorite charity have to win your favor every year for a donation? Does your country have to earn your devotion? You commit to some organizations, causes, and purposes just because you believe in them—their services, their products, their customers, their mission.

Motivate and Mentor Yourself

You hear it often, in tones of either dejection or astonishment: "My company doesn't even offer a mentoring program." Or, "This company doesn't even have a tuition-reimbursement plan." Being accountable means accepting responsibility for your own morale, motivation, and mobility. Identify what you don't know. Find out who can teach it to you. Ask others to let you observe and learn from them. Plan your educational road map, and be willing to pick up the tab. After all, you'll be reaping the benefits for the rest of your life.

Become Financially Savvy

Understand how a business works and how your own organization makes money. What are its expenses, and what generates its profits? How do you and your job alter the picture? Move around the organization and learn the same thing about every department in the organization: Do the people there cost money or make money for the team? How?

Focus on Your Own Deliverables and Forget about Others' To-Do Lists

Build your own integrity by delivering on your promises. Do what you say you will. Then stop grousing about others who don't meet deadlines or pull their own weight. They must live with the consequences of their lost clarity, diminished credibility, and damaged relationships.

Accept the Fact That Some Predicaments Don't Have Perfect Solutions

Instead of striving for perfection, settle for progress. Progress should happen on our watch—if only because it will transform and teach us how to cope in an imperfect situation.

Vow to Do Your Best with What You Have

Anyone can succeed with the right people, ample resources, appropriate support, and adequate time. Remove one of the legs from the stool, and you have a challenge worthy of your best talents. Measure your results by how well you accept and meet the challenge before you.

Live with Uncertainty

Stop expecting your leaders—organizational leaders, national leaders, world leaders—to read a crystal ball. Plan for tomorrow, but work within the parameters of today.

Signature Stars play their positions by being fully accountable for what happens on their watch and by assuming responsibility for results. Playing the blame game does not interest them. They prefer to take on the challenge of unpredictable situations under less-than-desirable circumstances and work to deliver dynamic results.

*W*hat have you not yet accepted full accountability for in your imperfect world?

*No individual raindrop ever considers itself responsible
for the flood.*   —UNKNOWN

✴ **As a Signature Star, Your Autograph Says You . . .**
Accept responsibility for results.

EIGHT

PLAY WITH THE REST
OF THE TEAM

All too often a basketball team with only one great scorer finds itself in trouble: The opponents double-team that star shooter, putting two defenders on her to inhibit shooting opportunities. Other teams start to scout the games and study that one scorer, and they focus all their effort on shutting down that one player's moves. Or worse, that star scorer may become injured or have a family emergency that makes her unavailable for a game or a whole season.

It's not necessarily the star scorer who hogs the ball. It may be the worst player on the team—the one the coach sends into the game with only two minutes to go and a twenty-eight-point lead. Someone passes her the ball, and she knows it'll probably be the only time she touches it all night. So she's not about to pass it off. She's determined to shoot from midcourt—even if she has three defenders trying to knock the ball out of her hands.

Even high scorers know that their success depends on

others—those who assist, rebound, defend, or steal the ball from the opponents.

The same is true at work: Your success sooner or later depends on other people, either substantively or minimally.

TEAMMATES PASS OFF TO YOU—OR NOT

Choice projects or assignments, or even promotions, may or may not come your way based on your track record and competence. Many times such decisions stem from your past performance "plus"—plus someone's personal recommendation that you're the right person for the project or job.

TEAMMATES MAY SET UP THE PLAY BY EITHER BLOCKING OR SCREENING

As you work, your job may grow easier or more difficult depending on how much help you receive from other people, departments, or divisions around you. They may either cooperate or drag their feet in returning phone calls, participating in meetings, supplying data, meeting deadlines, reviewing documents, releasing files, giving approvals.

In short, they can either run interference for you or be interference for you.

TEAMMATES MAY "REBOUND" YOUR WORK

If you miss your work goal and fail to deliver the expected results, your colleagues have the option of giving you a second chance— or not. They can toss the ball back to you and let you try again without any penalty except a little lost effort and time. Or, they can take your imperfect shot (results), improve on it, and then redirect it so that it scores the desired effect.

TEAMMATES "TALK YOU UP" TO THE FANS AND MEDIA

Peers at work "interpret" you to the rest of the marketplace—your stakeholders. They control how others view your work. Either you "did a great job" on X project, or you were "in over your head." Their opinions will be controlled largely by how well you've treated them.

TEAMMATES PROVIDE RELIEF

Sooner or later you'll need a replacement so you can accept a promotion and move up in the organization. Not having anyone trained to take their place limits many people's upward mobility. Even when you're talking not about promotions but about daily routines, the fact that you have a backup ready to play your position gives clients and coworkers a sense of comfort.

Gary took his team obligations seriously. When his female manager began having trouble integrating their computer systems in their office, upper management suggested that she or someone on her staff go back to school for an advanced degree in computer science. The manager had a one-year-old child and didn't want to compromise her parenting responsibilities to attend night school at the time. Gary volunteered to go back to school for the advanced degree, bringing the necessary technical expertise to the department. Two years later, when the manager moved on, she recommended Gary as her replacement.

Ultimately, your success depends on others. It has always been a strong work principle.

The church in New Testament times understood the value of playing as a team. Acts 6:1-7 recounts one of the first efforts to divide the responsibilities of church ministry. In order to allow the apostles to continue their preaching responsibilities without being burdened with other tasks, the church selected seven leaders to administer the distribution of food to the poor. Each of the leaders had a different role to play in accomplishing their mission. Paul, John Mark, and Barnabas served as the first missionary team, and later they paired off into two teams: Barnabas and John Mark as one and Paul and Silas as the other. Jesus and his disciples served as a team. Jesus took his team with him through his darkest days and hours, even asking them to watch and pray with him in the garden of Gethsemane.

So consider how you build your reputation as a team player at work: (1) Learn to see things from multiple viewpoints and interpret the benefit for the other parties involved. They don't want to know how you will benefit; they want to know how they will benefit. (2) Keep people informed of your plans every step of the way. People support what they help create; they want to feel a part of the process. (3) Share the credit for your success.

Playing with the rest of the team elevates your Signature Star status.

Would your coworkers see you as a team player or as someone who hogs the ball?

You can employ men and hire hands to work for you, but you must win their hearts to have them work with you.

—TIORIO

✶ **As a Signature Star, Your Autograph Says You . . .**
Become a team player.

NINE

TAKE YOUR SHOT

Imagine that you're the coach, and your team is leading by two points with two minutes to go in the game. Would you try to slow things down, hold the ball, play it safe? Or would you continue to play full speed ahead and try to widen your lead by another basket or two before the final buzzer? Your decision and rationale will probably stem from your natural inclination for risk taking.

People face the same decision—whether consciously or subconsciously—on the job. Typically, people who prefer to stall the ball fall into four categories:

Retired-on-the-Job People: These people go to work every day not to accomplish a mission, reach a goal, or deliver results but simply to put in their time.

"Yes" People: These workers have found it easier to "just say yes" to whatever someone proposes than to risk upsetting others by asking questions or expressing an opposing viewpoint. So they go along to get along.

Comfortable People: These people freeze the ball so they can enjoy their lead. They refuse to accept "stretch" assignments that would help them or their job to grow. They do not want to tackle anything that would challenge their feelings of competence and success.

Fearful People: These people hide out on the job. Their goal is to stay off everybody's radar screen. They move through their workweek thinking, *How can I accomplish X without making a mistake and calling undue attention to myself or this department?*

> *There are a lot of ways to become a failure, but never taking a chance is the most successful.* —UNKNOWN

Oren Harari, author of *The Powell Principles,* summarizes Colin Powell's observation about the link between risk taking and a manager's effectiveness: "Less effective middle managers tend to say, 'If I haven't explicitly been told *yes,* I can't do it.' The best ones tend to say, 'If I haven't explicitly been told *no,* I CAN do it.'"[1]

So why take your shot? Why play with an all-out, risk-acceptable effort?

RISKS MAKE WORK AND LIFE EXCITING

When you stop taking risks and putting forth your best effort, you extract the excitement from most jobs. But let's face it: Many people run in a rut—in life in general and in their work specifically.

Mac Irwin introduces new computer systems into companies to help people manage change. But Mac observes that even when the new systems he and his team install clearly help people do their jobs better, people resist the change initially. They prefer hanging on to the faulty familiar rather than reaching for the risky, untried, and unknown.

Even if things are boring, people prefer boring to change because boring is comfortable. We order the same entrée from the same favorite restaurant weekend after weekend. We buy the same brand of shoes season after season. We select the same car colors year after year. To many people, boring and bland are better than risk and results.

No one ever climbed a hill just by looking at it. —UNKNOWN

WITHOUT RISK, STAGNATION SETS IN

Every day that you're not moving forward, you're losing ground—in your skills, your product or service innovation, your technology, or your competitive advantage. Either you risk, you stretch, and you grow, or you rein in, you ruin, and you run slow.

That's not to say that if you have only a two-point lead and two minutes to play in the game, you're going to stand in center court and lob the ball toward the basket or take careless shots from the perimeter. But a great game calls for reasonable risks and thoughtful action. According to Elbert Hubbard, "The greatest mistake you will make in life is to be continually fearing you will make one."

Signature Stars take their shots. Don't let it be said of you or your work team, "They're not playing to win—they're playing not to lose."

*O*n your current assignments, are you playing to win or just running out the clock?

Don't be afraid to take a big step when one is indicated. You can't cross a chasm in two small jumps.

—DAVID LLOYD GEORGE

✳ **As a Signature Star, Your Autograph Says You . . .**
Accept calculated risks and take action.

TEN

ADMIT YOUR FOULS

The referee blows his whistle and yells, "Foul on number forty-two!" The player wearing jersey forty-two jerks his head around in disbelief with a "Who? Me?" glare as the opponent jogs toward the free-throw line.

If the opponent makes the free throws and racks up the extra points, the offending player's denial often grows worse. Number forty-two hangs his hands on his hips, wags his head, trots over to the sidelines to catch a few words with the coach about how he didn't go "within five feet of that guy." If the two free throws are enough to put the other team in the lead, you'll likely see even more foot stomping, head wagging, and mumbling—all forms of denial and disengagement.

Few people readily own up to the consequences of their actions—on the basketball court or at the office. Yet mistakes are a fact of work life, just as they are a fact of sports. As someone has aptly observed, if you're not making mistakes, you're either not trying hard enough or you're not on the cutting edge.

Mistakes generally fall into two categories—smart mistakes and stupid mistakes.

Smart mistakes are negative outcomes that result from decisions or actions based on calculated risks. In other words, you made the best decision you could in the circumstance at the time with the information you had. If the same situation occurred again, you would probably make the same decision.

Stupid mistakes are negative outcomes that result from faulty decisions or actions caused by poor judgment, ego, impatience, or inattention to detail. These errors should not have happened at all.

Just like mistakes, people's reactions to having made mistakes also fall into two categories: They either hold themselves accountable or deny responsibility for their actions. And they earn or lose respect from coworkers accordingly.

Without exception, every manager I interviewed could divide their colleagues and clients into these two camps: the it's-not-my-fault group and the I'm-responsible-for-the-results group.

> *Never fear criticism when you're right; never ignore criticism when you're wrong.*   —UNKNOWN

A human resources manager has two systems analysts in mind as she considers this issue. "One analyst, Barbara, absolutely won't admit a mistake. Anything that goes wrong is always a 'systems error' or the fault of the other person who 'miscommunicated.' She claims someone's raise didn't go through and that's why it didn't get on the current period's payroll. She's very defensive about any feedback.

"On the other hand, I have another systems analyst who

just made a horrendous error and readily admitted it. Her error
caused 185 people to be overpaid between $200 and $7,000 on
a particular pay period. We had to void all the checks and rerun
payroll for that period. That involved going to the employees
and asking them to return the money. If they didn't give it
back, we had to withhold it from the next paycheck. It took us
four months, six human resources staffers, and two VPs to get
it all straightened out. But she owned up to it. And she kept
her job."

Two analysts with two different attitudes: The first says,
"I'm not accountable for anything that goes wrong"; the second,
"I'm responsible for accuracy."

Ken Harbin, former oil executive, often saw both kinds
in the oil patches around the world: "I recall drilling a well in
West Texas as a result of a group decision at corporate. Our
intention was to get a pipeline unstuck, but it resulted in a
blowout. The superintendent in charge was quick to come
in and say, 'We did the wrong thing.' He assumed the responsibility for the blowout, when the initial decision to drill wasn't
even his.

"But in another situation in Yemen, we had an employee
who let a well get out of control because of a very stupid mistake—a very small detail, just not thinking of the proper type of
wellhead to use. Over there, they use several different types, and
each type calls for a different procedure. He'd worked on the
well two weeks earlier, so he knew the type, but just didn't think.
We had to fly in three experts from the U.S. to control the fire
at a cost of half a million dollars. It was habitual with him to
be careless and cavalier about errors. The president fired him."

Admitting mistakes doesn't shield you from the consequences. And sometimes you reap good results in spite of mistakes. But consequences or not, readily admitting mistakes and being willing to correct them does earn respect.

Tim Alba recounts one of his first meetings with the CEO of his organization, where he'd been hired a few months earlier as corporate controller. The CEO was reviewing some invoices and checks that Tim's staff had written and found a check for $1,000 that didn't match an invoice. The CEO glanced up and questioned him on the expenditure.

Tim looked over the entry and finally responded, "I don't know what this is. I can't explain it. Obviously, I missed something."

The CEO smiled. "Tim, you and I are going to get along just fine." The CEO moved on and never mentioned the error again.

Now that Tim has been in this position for years and has learned the culture, he understands well the meaning of that remark, as he did that day. His employer values integrity and a straightforward answer—even if it's "I blew it." Tim follows the same principle: "Tell me. Don't spin me."

Ironically, the person you can trust to look you square in the eye and say, "I messed up," is the person you can trust with bigger responsibilities.

Karen Rinehart, too, learned early on that acknowledging errors tends to build, rather than destroy, trust with superiors. While working for a major oil and gas company, she amended a gas contract that actually needed no amendment. (The oil wells in question were already covered under the current contract, but she did not interpret the legal description correctly.) As a result, the amendment specified current gas prices rather than twenty-year-old gas prices. Her error cost the company $100,000. When she discovered her mistake and reported it to her boss, he responded, "You've saved us that much and more on other contracts. What did you learn from this mistake?" She never heard from him again on the matter.

An important reason to admit your shortcomings and mistakes is growth. As King David learned during his lifetime by responding to his mistakes and sins with a contrite heart and humility, it's hard to learn from errors that you don't acknowledge making. Responsible people admit their wrongs.[1]

A second reason to own up to shortcomings and mistakes is that others forgive much more readily then than when you try to deny them. Another statement from the book of Proverbs says, "People who cover over their sins will not prosper. But if they confess and forsake them, they will receive mercy."[2] By "prospering," the writer of Proverbs is saying that you will learn from your mistakes and grow, and by "mercy" you will receive forgiveness. Denying your fouls leads others to continue to blow their referee's whistle louder and louder. All you need to do to verify this biblical truth is observe public reaction to political faux pas and sins of our elected officials. Acknowledging the mistake—even when the error is egregious—typically quiets the noise.

Acknowledge errors. Learn from them. Accept consequences. Move on down the court and play ball.

*H*ow readily do you own up to your fouls: when fitting or only when you're forced to?

*When the most insignificant person tells us we are in error,
we should listen, and examine ourselves, and see if it is so.
To believe it possible we may be in error, is the first step
toward getting out of it.*   —JOHANN K. LAVATER

✴ **As a Signature Star, Your Autograph Says You . . .**
Admit your errors.

ELEVEN

WORK FOR THE GOOD
OF THE TEAM

Let's say you're the coach of a new college ball team. Your time
and travel funds are limited, so you need to cut a few players.
During the first several practice sessions you plan to watch the
team work out to decide which players to keep and which to cut.

As you watch them shoot baskets, run drills, and scrimmage,
you see that they're all competent and skilled in the fundamentals. But you observe the following during the first two weeks at
training camp:

- Player 16 arrives an hour early for every session
  to shoot baskets.
- Player 20 stays a half hour late after every session
  to run extra laps.
- Player 86 misses two practices because of "prior
  commitments."
- Player 44 encourages other team members when
  they make mistakes.
- Player 63 expresses discontent with the amount of time

he's allowed to scrimmage in comparison with other, less-seasoned players.

- Player 46 volunteers to set up a call roster for parents who might want to trade referrals for travel arrangements to the out-of-town games.
- Player 88 complains frequently that the uniform colors are outdated.
- Player 50 stays late four out of five sessions to study scrimmage tapes.
- Player 82 calls the hospital to ask about injured players every morning before he shows up for practice and reports to the rest of the team members about their condition.
- Player 52 routinely takes personal cell-phone calls in the middle of practice.
- Player 58 leaves trash on the floor of the locker room for the cleaning crew.
- Player 74 invites personal friends to stop by and have lunch with him from the team buffet and never offers to pick up the tab.
- Player 49 refuses to talk to other players or pass on information they obviously missed when they arrive late, leave early, or are off the court momentarily for other reasons.

How would these observations affect your choices about who gets cut and who stays on the team? whom you would trust to serve and lead the others to peak performance?

The executive of the future will be rated by his ability
to anticipate his problems rather than to meet them
as they come.   —HOWARD COONLEY

Observations of those around us at work seem equally clear. The following comments make it easy to spot those who think like an owner/coach and those who don't:

Those Who Think Like Owners/ Coaches (as described by their coworkers or bosses)	Those Who Don't (as described by their coworkers or bosses)
"A Dallas high-rise caught fire when the electrical service blew up. Our electrician went in at 4 A.M., took charge, and evacuated the building. Although he wasn't officially 'in charge,' he got six to eight people working on it, and they worked straight through for three days. Others accepted delegated tasks from him because he kept working on it himself until it was completed."	"This particular nurse never asked probing questions when people called about their insurance coverage. She just answered, 'It's not covered' about questionable situations. Then someone else on our staff always had to call the insurance company to find out the patient's benefits and verify coverage. She never tried to work by time zone on the East Coast to get as many answers for patients as she could by closing time. She just called to verify 'in the order they were dropped in her box.' And yet people were seriously ill, waiting for emergency surgery, and trying to verify their coverage!"
"She sent her own kids to the vacation Bible school in T-shirts advertising the academy. We're looking for ways to let the community know we exist and spread the word to increase our enrollment. She knew we needed to use whatever inexpensive means possible to advertise."	"We're a parochial school with continual cash-flow issues. I watched a parent walk up to our window to pay his child's tuition. The person behind the window had it closed. He knocked on the window, and she wouldn't open it. He finally gave up and said, 'I guess I'll go home and mail it.' And we needed the money quickly!"
"When she went to the new company, she discovered they had no job aids to help new employees get acclimated. So she created them on the job and left them for other employees."	"Anthena took coffee supplies home for family gatherings because she said it was only right since she didn't drink her fair share of coffee at the office."
"We had a patient who'd had a cardiac catheterization and an irregular heartbeat. He was on a monitor for observation, and an inexperienced nurse came on shift to relieve Karen at the end of her duty. The new nurse didn't know what to do, so Karen was afraid to leave her with the patient. She stayed a second shift with the new nurse."	"I worked with a guy who made so many personal calls that they set up an account for him and started billing them back to him. They just withheld the charges from his paycheck. I don't know how he got any work done."

"Frey Rad was seventeen when he came to the U.S., very dedicated, industrious. He was always coming up with recommendations to acquire another company or property for drilling. He worked over Thanksgiving weekend to do a proposal requesting $30 million to acquire property for a project. I could call him today and say, 'I need $5,000 tomorrow,' and he'd put it in the mail to me. He became a Christian early in his midtwenties and has a strong work ethic. I took him with me to three different companies as a reservoir engineer."	"This particular manager of one of our retail centers was stable but not ambitious. Just lazy. Even though we pay extra for overtime, this manager would turn down business if he had to stay fifteen minutes late to wait on a customer or to wait for a driver to make an extra delivery. He was holding back operations. Another person in the center saw the potential and raised the bar beyond the management's leadership there—verbally and by example."
"Dean worked with us before starting his own business. But even back before he refined a new hot sauce and started packaging it, you could tell he was going to be successful. High energy. Creative. He showed the same traits in the insurance business. Handled high volume. Came up with creative client solutions."	
"Sandy Delter saved this huge development project—$750,000—from going down the drain at Nissan. It was off track because the various parties weren't talking to each other, and the vendor couldn't get the necessary user data. The manager's neck was on the line. But she took charge of it—even though it wasn't part of her job. She collected the data internally and handed it over to the vendor so they could finish development. And her action saved this huge project for the company."	
"Sylvia Dubach handles janitorial crews and less technical parts of daily operations. When we were working the Christmas holidays to move people from Seattle, she showed up—even though she had laryngitis and a bad sinus infection. She was outside helping unload these 18-wheelers, supervising crews, writing notes and sticking them in front of the crews, telling them where to put the equipment and furniture. We kept telling her to go home because she was really sick. This was completely beyond her job scope. The senior executives and truck drivers were totally impressed."	

"Karim spoke French and Arabic. He spent personal time with Arabic leaders in the community just to develop rapport with them. So when problems developed between our company and the local government officials in their country, he was able to resolve them quickly and easily. That was not really his official job. He just took it upon himself."

So what's common among those people mentioned in the left-hand column? People who think like owners and coaches

- expend the energy
- put in the time
- go to the trouble
- probe to gain information
- learn what's new
- spread the word
- volunteer for what needs to be done
- take charge
- set the standard for others
- model the example
- delegate to get things done
- work alongside others
- stay until it's over
- bring people together
- think nothing of it

People who think like owners or coaches see the big picture and put the common good above self-interest. As a result, they earn the respect of their team.

*I*f you were one of the players in the college-team lineup mentioned at the chapter opening, which jersey number would you be wearing? Or would you be the coach?

You have to expect things of yourself before you can do them.

—MICHAEL JORDAN

✳ As a Signature Star, Your Autograph Says You . . .
Work for the common good.

TWELVE

PLAY BY THE RULES

Have you ever played a game of driveway basketball, three on three, when the group makes up the rules as you go? Rocks, sticks, or old shoes typically serve as the boundary lines, and the markers often get moved during the course of the game. What's going to be the rule about bringing the ball into play after a basket? Does the opposing team have to dribble it back across the half-court marker before they can shoot it, or can they take a shot immediately as they bring it into play? What are you going to do about fouls? Are you going to have a three-point line, or is every goal a two-pointer?

If you happen to take such a game seriously, the rules that evolve on such short notice can prove to be sources of contention.

Likewise at work. When people decide to disregard the Bible as their moral compass and official business handbook, they begin to make up the rules as they go. Anything can happen, and the situation frequently proves to be a source of contention.

Since the rash of high-profile cases ranging from Enron to WorldCom to Arthur Andersen to Tyco to Merrill Lynch

to Martha Stewart to American Airlines to the New York Times
to Boeing, our attention has been focused on business ethics.
The trade journal *Publishers Weekly* surveyed the publishing
industry for the hottest topics of the 2003–2004 season and
discovered all major book publishers bringing out books on
business ethics, certainly a reflection of a gaping need in the
fabric of our society.

> *A people that values its privileges above its principles soon
> loses both.*   —DWIGHT D. EISENHOWER

But business morality hasn't been left to the books. These recent
corporate scandals have generated other attempts to provide a
moral compass: The accrediting agency for the nation's univer-
sity-level business schools has put universities on notice that
an ethics curriculum will become part of the accreditation review
process. However, according to reactions around the country
from university officials, either such curriculum has been in
place for years and has made little difference in behavior, or
university deans plan to add such courses, with the expectation
that students' ethics have already been shaped by parents long
before they enter the university.[1]

But it's not like this is the first time people have heard of ethics
in the workplace. The Society for Human Resource Management
says 79 percent of all companies already have written ethics standards. And just in case people still don't get the picture, many are
now hiring "ethics officers" or "business practices officers" or "vice
presidents of compliance and integrity." The Ethics Officers Association started in 1992 with 12 members and now has more than
950 members representing 500 companies.

So has all the attention solved the problem? No, not if you consider the latest crime statistics.

The Global Economic Crime Survey (produced by the law firm of Wilmer, Cutler & Pickering in association with PricewaterhouseCoopers)[2] found that 37 percent of U.S. corporations experienced significant crimes. Asset misappropriation (25 percent of the crimes) and cyber crimes (8 percent) surfaced as the most prevalent types.

Several years ago, Karen Drake was dismayed to find herself up close and personal with white-collar crime in a five-week job for a home-health-care system. She'd been pleased to find the job for a "Christian" manager, who held Bible studies every morning before work and said that God had called him from the oil field to the health-care field to improve people's lives. Quickly, she discovered the organization was fraudulently billing Medicare for unused supplies and services not rendered. She conferred with another nurse there, who confirmed that the fraudulent practice had been going on for a long time and agreed to go with Karen to report it to the business owner.

When Karen wrote her letter of resignation and traveled to a distant city to report the situation to the owner, he offered to hire her as a quality-assurance consultant who would go back to the office and identify all the discrepancies. She accepted the job—only to discover that the owner was working behind her to "fix the charts" and using her "quality assurance" work only to identify the errors that needed "fixing." She promptly left the organization a second time and reported the practice to the nursing board—but not without serious personal consequences: trauma over the incident and unemployment.

This is but one example of the kind of moral dilemmas and

their consequences workers face routinely when they decide to play by the rule book. Other situations can be less clear-cut.

Take Kevin's situation at a large computer company during a massive layoff. His region is being lopped off. At the director level, he has a choice to save his own job during the cutback: Option 1—He can bid for another job in another region in a highly competitive situation. If he loses, he's off the payroll altogether and out the door. Option 2—He can bump one of his four direct reports out of a job and take it for himself.

His decision? His direct reports have all done excellent work and have given him no reason to remove them from their position. He chooses option 1, based on doing the right thing—which is usually one step above the ethical thing, which is usually one step above the legal thing.

As much as we may like to make up our own rules on occasion, God has already given us the rule book. If we're going to play or ref in the real world, we'd do well to read it.

*H*ow comfortable would you be with the paparazzi following you around at work for the next six months? Would you need to change the rules of engagement with any of your suppliers, clients, contractors, or colleagues?

No man has a right to do as he pleases, except when he pleases to do right.   —CHARLES SIMMONS

✴ **As a Signature Star, Your Autograph Says You . . .**
Do the right, ethical thing.

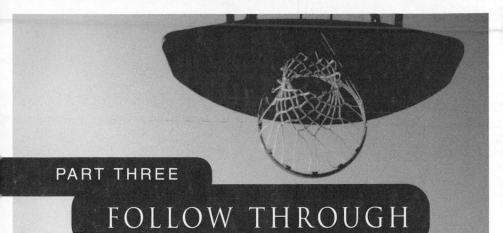

PART THREE

FOLLOW THROUGH

*M*any people dream rather than deliver.

In their business best seller *Execution,* Larry Bossidy and Ram Charan point out the alarming trend of CEOs of the Fortune 500 being fired or forced to resign—a trend they predict will continue for some time. The reason? Not for lack of grand visions and plans. Not for lack of innovative products or services. Not for lack of dedicated staff around them. Not for ethical or moral failures. Despite all they have going for them, the common failure among those at the top is their inability to execute their plans.

The weakness can be traced all the way to the lowest ranks in an organization—the department manager motivating new staff, the team leader training new people, the project manager scheduling work, the account executive handling a sale, the consultant coordinating a client project, the administrative assistant arranging a staff meeting, the customer-service agent investigating a problem, the shipping clerk packing an order.

Points go on the scoreboard only when the ball goes through the hoop.

THIRTEEN

FIND CHEERLEADERS

As long as you're shooting baskets in the driveway or gym alone, you can lie to yourself about how many you make—or even how many shots you take. Did you shoot 200 baskets? Or was it only 175? Did you make 65 out of 100 free throws? Or was it only 55? Did you run ten laps after practice or was it only nine? If no one knows your intentions and plans, then probably no one cares if you accomplished what you set out to do.

No accountability, no embarrassment, . . . and no progress.

You've probably known people who can "talk a good game" at work but never seem to play one. They make excellent analysts— of everyone else's plans and results. One CEO talks of members on one of the executive committees of his professional association: "Frank always comes with a list of things 'they' should have done. So the committee typically puts him on the task force to correct the problem. Then six months down the road at the next meeting, when they ask what he's ready to do, it's always 'still under advisement.' He's good at telling other people what they've 'missed.' But he can never help follow through with the plans to correct the situation. He changes jobs every few years, and my guess is that's why."

You may recognize yourself as one of those people whose strength is coming up with great ideas, but whose weakness is an inability to execute. Although great plans excite people, the lack of execution frustrates them, as these comments from staff indicate:

- "This particular executive would go away to a seminar and then come back to us: 'All sixteen branches—do this and make it work.' Then he'd never reinforce it or implement it or follow through with any specific plans or support systems, but just go on to the next fad."

- "We used to have Profit Suggestion Teams: People won awards for ideas and got all kinds of gifts, bonuses, and so forth. But no one ever was assigned to implement the ideas."

- "We have meetings at the end of the year to generate ideas for great fund-raisers. My boss and her team would come up with fantastic ideas to generate community support and earn sponsorships. This last year it was a big tennis tournament—bring in big-name players. But she never did any of them."

- "Jorge has a reputation for big ideas. He's always saying, 'Let's do a big research project on user attitude toward this or that equipment.' The idea is that we'll use it for marketing purposes—do a big press release to the industry and so forth. It's his job to sell the idea to our senior executives and get the funding. But he can never get it done—just never gets around to it."

No accountability. No encouragement. No progress.

Aside from tips and techniques, two big reasons for coaches and personal trainers in the sports world are accountability and encouragement. They expect you to show up, work hard, and do what you say you will. In fact, business coaching has become one of the hottest new occupations of the last few years. The International Coach Federation, formed in 1996, now boasts more than 6,000 members and has three levels of certification. Having a personal business coach has become a status symbol. But a supervisor, colleague, or team leader can provide accountability and encouragement as well.

It's easier to follow through when you have someone watching. So get these cheerleaders in your corner:

Cheerleaders help you identify your strengths and remind you to use them. Cheerleaders and coaches in your corner of the court help you to assess your skills and determine what position you'd play best. Are you fast on your feet? How's your jump shot? Are you tall enough to play center? Are you a threat from behind the arc? Do you have an accurate hook shot?

Cheerleaders enjoy seeing star players execute plays based on their strengths. For example, they'll often come up with chants customized to a specific player. Think of some of the great players down through the years: If their team was three points behind, the Boston Celtics crowd began to chant for them to give the ball to Larry Bird, famous for shooting from behind the arc for the three-point bonanza. The Lakers cheerleaders yelled for Kareem Abdul-Jabbar to take his hook shot. The Houston Rockets fans encouraged Hakeem Olajuwon to do his dream shake. Michael Jordan fans cheered to see him jump up in midair and get a shot off from just about anywhere.

Your cheerleaders at work serve the same function. Bosses, team leaders, or mentors can help you identify your strengths and then put you in positions or on projects that allow you to use those strengths to shine.

Cheerleaders warn you of trouble ahead. Coaches also help you work on your weaknesses to ward off problems before they develop. Do you need to improve the accuracy of your free throws? Are you slow on rebounds? Do you need better control in your running game? They design drills and scrimmages to help you improve in these areas.

Cheerleaders also warn of trouble from the outside. If your team is behind and you need to get off the winning shot, you'll hear the cheerleaders chant, "Watch the clock. Watch the clock." If the other team intercepts a pass and makes a fast break for their goal, you'll hear the crowd shout, "Get down court. Cover her. Get down court!" If the other team is ahead and begins to dribble the ball to run out the clock, you'll hear the cheerleaders shout, "Foul 'em—stop the clock! Foul 'em—stop the clock!"

Your cheerleaders at work serve you in these same ways. They identify skills that need to be strengthened and help you set up action plans and gain stretch assignments to grow in those areas. With your projects and plans that may be in jeopardy, they point out trouble spots and suggest check-back points for further direction.

> *Refuse good advice and watch your plans fail; take good counsel and watch them succeed.*
>
> —PROVERBS 15:22, *THE MESSAGE*

Cheerleaders rally the crowd to support your efforts. Spectators have their own way of "watching" a game. Some walk the stands to visit with friends. Some spend half their time at the concession stands, buying hot dogs and popcorn. Some pick up dates. Some argue with the refs over bad calls. Some chase their misbehaving children. Some conduct business with their clients. But when the cheerleaders start a yell, most conversations get drowned out and people tune in, at least momentarily, to what's happening on the court. They focus their full attention on your efforts.

Cheerleaders at work serve the same function. They bring together all the various players who must contribute to your project, process, or task and get them behind your effort. Understandably, others get sidetracked in their own dramas at work. And their failure to meet a deadline, provide data, give a callback, or attend a meeting can jeopardize your ability to execute your plans.

This is where your cheerleader comes in. Although you hope to use personal power as often as possible, knowing that you're accountable to someone else to execute your plan can make the difference in your commitment to drive the project to completion. It's not that you'd have to call on your coach to intervene; it's the fact that you've made a commitment to that coach that often provides your own impetus to execute.

Cheerleaders build your confidence. Cheerleaders place their faith in you to accomplish your mission. The entire crowd yelling for you to succeed starts the adrenaline pumping and inspires you to believe in yourself.

Cheerleaders at work inspire the same confidence. Committing to someone else in writing that you will accomplish X by Y date and having them believe in you strongly enough to take their own action steps based on your word starts the game clock.

Cheerleaders celebrate your wins with you. Having cheerleaders slap you on the back after a win with "Great game!" feels much better than watching them walk away with head down and hearing them mumble, "Better luck next time." The apostle Paul envisioned such a crowd of cheerleaders in the faithful crowd of believers who have preceded us to heaven and are watching from the grandstands: "Do you see what this means—all these pioneers who blazed the way, all the veterans cheering us on? It means we'd better get on with it. Strip down, start running—and never quit!"[1] They expected him to celebrate his accomplished mission on earth, and he gained inspiration looking forward to the party!

Your cheerleaders at work will expect you to win. And that's the idea. Depending on their role relative to yours in the organization, they will find their job much easier. Their project will click. Their stress will decrease. Their stock will rise. Is it any wonder they want you to execute?

*W*ho are your cheerleaders, encouraging you and holding you accountable for results?

_____

> *People may doubt what you say, but they will always*
> *believe what you do.*   —UNKNOWN

_____

✷ **As a Signature Star, Your Autograph Says You . . .**
Commit to others who will hold you accountable
and encourage you to execute your plans.

FOURTEEN

DEVELOP A PLAYBOOK

Both offense and defense call for planning. On defense, teams typically adopt either a zone pattern or play person-to-person coverage. Offensive planning gets more complex: Who passes off to whom, who screens, who fakes and dribbles back out, who tosses to center, or who charges in for the layup.

If you want to execute like a well-oiled machine during a game, you develop the plays. You memorize the plays. You practice the plays. You run the plays.

Hope isn't a plan.

God did his work in the world in an orderly fashion with a plan.[1] Some of God's most successful servants on assignment in the Bible had a plan: Joseph had a plan to lead the Egyptians through the seven years of famine.[2] Nehemiah had a plan to rebuild the temple.[3] Esther had a plan to save her nation from annihilation.[4] Paul had a plan as he conducted his missionary journeys.[5]

Not only does the Bible speak of strategic planning, it also speaks of project planning: "Suppose one of you wants to build a tower. Will he not first sit down and estimate the cost to see if he has enough money to complete it? For if he lays the foundation and is not able to finish it, everyone who sees it will ridicule him, saying, 'This fellow began to build and was not able to finish.'"[6] David had a plan to rebuild the temple—a plan that he says God put directly in his mind in great detail.[7]

> *Let our advance worrying become advance thinking and planning.*   —WINSTON CHURCHILL

The book of Proverbs, too, advises about the importance of planning: "The wise look ahead to see what is coming,"[8] and "A prudent person foresees the danger ahead and takes precautions; the simpleton goes blindly on and suffers the consequences."[9] And another: "Be sure you know the condition of your flocks, give careful attention to your herds."[10] In other words, stay in touch with what's going on in your business.

For many organizations, departments, and teams, their planning equates to meetings. And meetings. And more meetings. All without action. Planning, however, involves more than just talking.

> *You can't build a reputation on what you're going to do.*   —HENRY FORD

Excessive talking, in fact, can be dangerous to delivery. Enthusiasm wanes as you talk and talk and talk. With the excitement stripped away, all that's left is the actual work. Rather than get the payoff of praise from the finished project, you get the payoff from the ooh-and-aah effect of the promises. That makes execut-

ing the actual plans much less exciting—and much less likely
to get done.

> Good plans shape good decisions. That's why good planning
> helps to make elusive dreams come true.   —LESTER R. BITTEL

Another primary pitfall about planning involves plunging
off the deep end without prayer. Planning without asking for
God's guidance often leads to frustration and even disaster.
"Trust in the Lord with all your heart; do not depend on your
own understanding. Seek his will in all you do, and he will
direct your paths."[11]

To execute well as a Signature Star, get specific about your
mission and then work backward: Pray for direction. Set your
goal. Identify major deadlines and interim deadlines. Identify
the resources needed. Agree on criteria of completion and
measures of success or failure. Pinpoint pitfalls that may cause
trouble, and develop precautionary measures. Schedule the
work. Then work your plan.

*D*o you have a playbook to consistently and quickly move
the ball down the court? Do you use it?

> The value of an idea lies in using it.   —THOMAS A. EDISON

✳ **As a Signature Star, Your Autograph Says You . . .**
Plan rather than talk.

FIFTEEN

PRACTICE THE WAY YOU INTEND TO PLAY

Doing the drill *correctly* is the deal. If you do it carelessly, you might as well quit. The coach tosses the ball toward the backboard. The first player in line jumps to meet the ball midair and bats it back against the board. The second player jumps to meet the ball and bats it back against the board. Then the third player takes her turn, and so forth in rapid succession, without letting the ball hit the floor. But let a player wait for the ball to come down and meet her hands without jumping for it and she has missed the point of the drill. It's not about batting the ball to the backboard; it's about meeting the ball in the air.

Total failure. Missing that one key detail of the drill will mean that the player fails to learn how to rebound effectively. Come game time, she's going to repeat that incorrect maneuver and stand flat-footed, making it easier for the opponent to take the ball away from her. Mishandled details leading to faulty follow-through can be caused by either systems problems or attitude problems. Either the coach isn't tossing the ball high

enough on the backboard so that the player has to jump
to rebound it—or the player doesn't care to.

The old adage "You'll play like you practice" is equally true
in the workforce. Inattention to details can stem from a mind-
set or a system problem.

A senior executive talks about two different staffers with
very different mind-sets: "Sherrie is careless. Her goal is to get
something checked off her to-do list. She doesn't care if it's
done right—just get it done. We had this huge mailing to go
out, inviting clients to attend a big conference in Hawaii. Thousands of pieces. She got the wrong dates and the wrong times
in the brochure. When questioned about the error, her response
was, 'Oh, well, most people don't pay attention to the first mailing anyway.'

"On the other hand, I'm totally impressed with the conven-
tion services manager at a hotel we regularly use in Houston for
these large conferences. I arrived in town for our meeting and
called her in a panic when I didn't see our executive breakfast
meeting listed on the contract. It's our most important meeting.

"'Mary, where's our breakfast meeting tomorrow?'

"She said, 'It's in the Nevada Room.'

"We had failed to tell her we needed the room. Although she
had three conventions going on, because she had worked with
us before and knew we always scheduled such a meeting, she had
reserved that room for us automatically. Details. She had a grasp
of the details and she cared about doing a good job."

> *There have been few successful men who weren't good at*
> *details. Don't ignore details. Lick them.*
>
> —WILLIAM B. GIVEN JR.

Whether lack of procedures or poor attitude causes foul-ups when people fail to get the details right, both situations can spell disaster:

- "We were involved in an environmental analysis for a court case where an organization was dumping chemicals in the lake. Francesca had pulled the sample and filled out the chain-of-custody tag on it, but she failed to transfer it to the log-in book for the court evidence. And that just happened to be one of the random pieces of evidence the judge asked to review. But because Francesca didn't log the sample into this book according to procedures, this critical piece of evidence—our very best piece of documented evidence to win the case—couldn't be used in court. As a result, we lost the case against this lawbreaking company."

- "My executive officer failed to do map reconnaissance on the road he planned to bring troops in on. He discovered the road wasn't there—it was woods! He was looking at an incorrect map. The guns were four hours late getting into position. Critical problem. We had troops left uncovered."

- "We had an employee drill a well using the wrong surveyor's stake as a marker. I told him it looked too close, but he insisted he was correct. It cost us $200,000 to drill that well and we didn't need it in that location at all! The well we had there was sufficient."

- "We developed a prototype software program for use in the U.S. and marketed it in Europe. Couldn't get it to work with a key client there, and the relationship got really tense. . . . I sent someone over to work on the problem and we discovered that someone had set it up in the U.S. date

format—month/day—versus the UK format—day/month.
That had kept the data from going into their system.
The person just never followed up on the small details."

- "Electricians install things and then fail to verify that what
they install actually works. It's the biggest problem we
have."

Getting the details right marks the difference between success
and failure at almost any level in almost any venture.

Mastery of the details leads to mastery of the big picture.
Many a bad decision and faulty policy can be traced to missed
or distorted details. Drop your attention to them and you distort
your view of a situation and damage your results. That is not to
say you should succumb to analysis paralysis or micromanage-
ment. It is to say that details well handled, under control, and
stacked end to end dictate your success on the major mission.

*D*o you master the details?

---

*If you are going to achieve excellence in big things, you
develop the habit in little matters.*   —COLIN POWELL

✶ **As a Signature Star, Your Autograph Says You . . .**
Get the details right.

SIXTEEN

SCRIMMAGE

"We've got our first scrimmage." Players love to hear those words from the coach because scrimmages are much more fun than squat thrusts, windmills, or shoulder and hip rotations. Scrimmaging is as close to a real game as you can get without the hoopla. And that's both a positive and a negative. The praise for performance doesn't mean as much—but neither does the pain of mistakes hurt so badly.

Scrimmaging serves multiple functions on the court and at work, all of which help you perform better in the regular season.

Scrimmaging trains you to think on your feet. You can do deep knee bends and squats, push-ups, and jumping jacks until you faint from exhaustion. You can pass, dribble figure eights, rebound from the boards, and sink free throws until you perfect the basics. But the real test is maneuvering with poise and purpose against your opponents. A scrimmage gives you opportunity to react appropriately to whatever unfolds on the court. You have the flexibility to run the best play to suit the situation.

At work, scrimmaging serves the same purpose. You need

opportunity to train before getting in the game. Many people fail to follow through with tasks for the simple reason that they've had no training. They're handed their equipment, told to suit up, and sent out to face the project or customer without a single scrimmage. Is it any wonder they can't think on their feet when faced with a tough situation? Result: They drop the ball and fail to follow through.

> *Knowledge is a treasure, but practice is the key to it.*
> —THOMAS FULLER

Scrimmaging provides a safe structure. The score doesn't count on the season record. In fact, you often play your own teammates—first string against second string. When that's the case, you may not even keep up with the time or the fouls. Instead, your attention is on the training—what happened, what didn't happen, what to do next time to make it happen.

At work, going without a scrimmage can be costly. You may have heard this story often told about a manager who hesitated to train his people: "What if I spend time, money, and effort to train my staff and they leave?" To which the consultant replied, "That's a problem. But what if you don't train them—and they stay?"

When you're in training, you can repeat a task or process and ask questions until you learn to do things right—before you lose a customer, damage your equipment, blow up a plant, or cause a lawsuit.

Scrimmaging allows replays until you get it right. You can stop in the middle of play without an okay from a referee and work on your technique. If you didn't handle the screen appropriately, the coach can have you run the play again. And again. And again. If you didn't get the ball after the tip-off, the coach can show you how he or she wants you to position yourself around the circle. Then you can try it again. And again.

Learning at work must be a continuous mind-set. Those at the top know the value of always expanding their skill set. Whether facing mergers or acquisitions, recruiting for top slots, opening new markets, or developing new product lines, senior executives analyze, study, and bring in consultants to do the replays of what their own staff has recommended—just to make sure they are getting it right before making the final game move. The habit of replays should trickle down until everybody gets it right.

What you knew last month has become outdated. Continual learning is the competitive advantage.

> *The will to win is worthless if you don't have the will to prepare.*   —THANE YOST

Scrimmaging builds bench strength. Scrimmaging keeps everybody on their toes. For the second stringers, it's their opportunity to go one-on-one with the first-string players, let the coach see how much their skills have improved, and win a place on the starting lineup for the next game. As a first stringer, this is not the time to relax because someone else is itching to take your place. If you're not playing at your best, you can quickly find yourself back on the bench.

Scrimmaging at work with "lesser" tasks on stretch assignments provides perfect opportunities to increase your skills and experience so that you're ready to take on more responsibility. Star managers make it a priority to build bench strength among the entire team—rather than depending on one or two stars in the department.

Scrimmaging instills confidence for the real game. If the play works well in scrimmage, chances are that it'll work in the game. If you make eighteen out of twenty hook or jump shots during scrimmage, chances are that you'll have the confidence to take your shots in the game. A successful scrimmage leads to a successful game.

The apostle Paul understood the value of self-discipline and training when he used the metaphor of training as an athlete for his mission: "Do you not know that in a race all the runners run, but only one gets the prize? Run in such a way as to get the prize. Everyone who competes in the games goes into strict training."[1]

> *It is more important to motivate your players for practice than for games.*   —JACK STALLINGS

Training and other professional-growth opportunities at work instill confidence—in you, your boss, your coworkers, your customers—and lead to success. The more skills you master, the more value you can contribute.

*H*ow often do you scrimmage in educational settings? How seriously do you scrimmage—does it make a difference in how you play ball in the real game?

_____

> *Sweat more in training and bleed less in battle.*   —UNKNOWN

_____

★ **As a Signature Star, Your Autograph Says You . . .**
Train—continuously improve your own skills and build the bench strength of your team.

SEVENTEEN

KNOW YOUR STATS

Ask professional basketball players their stats, and they can tell
you: Games per season. Minutes per game. Percentage of goals
made. Percentage of three-pointers. Percentage of free throws.
Offensive rebounds. Defensive rebounds. Assists per game. Steals
per game. Blocks per game. Turnovers per game. Personal fouls.
Average points per game. Similarly, a coach can furnish the stats
on the entire team as a whole, plus wins, losses, and injuries.

Anyone who's serious in their sport knows their stats. They
benchmark with the best and monitor their performance. To raise
your own work performance, you can use the same approach.
Identify the important stats, benchmark against the best in your
field, and compete against yourself. Let's get more specific.

Identify the important stats. The president of a publicly traded
equipment and services company had a frank discussion with
one of his senior managers about the value of waiting time.
Though an otherwise conscientious employee, this particular
senior manager habitually arrived about twenty minutes late
every morning and then kept his staff of mechanics waiting for

their daily assignments while he "grabbed a cup of coffee" and planned out their day.

One morning the president sat him down to do a little math—the cost of twenty minutes waiting time for X mechanics while they waited for their assignments. It was a real eye-opener for the manager. He had never calculated his staff's hourly cost so he didn't know what it cost him to hold a staff meeting, to close the service bay an hour early, to have three mechanics out sick—or to lose customer paperwork and spend ten minutes searching for it.

In your own area of responsibility, do you know what the important stats are? Is it cost per worker hours? Cost per packages shipped? Cost per mailing? Profit per widget sold? Accuracy of customer orders pulled from the warehouse? Average revenue loss due to under-billing errors on invoices? Number of calls handled by each customer-service agent per day? Days on outstanding receivables? Fuel efficiency per vehicle? Repairs handled per day? Number of sales calls made per week?

Not knowing your important stats is like not knowing the value of nickels, dimes, and dollars as a shopper.

Have a purpose for the data you collect. Know what's hot and what's not. Don't get bogged down in record-keeping just for the sake of record-keeping. Ask yourself, "Why do I need to get better with this?" "Will a minute or two make a significant difference here?" "Is saving three cents per widget an important differentiator?" "How much more speed will make a real difference to my customer?"

We have a client in the utility industry that we've been helping with communication issues. In the course of that consulting project, we've seen study after study of data they collected on

themselves about internal operating efficiencies in past years.
When I questioned them on how they're using the various data,
the executive vice president responded that he doesn't know
exactly, that they want it "just in case." From my observations
and conversations with four executives in the division, that
ongoing data collection has become enormously expensive not
to be useful.

Know what you're going to do with the data that you collect
to help you reach your ideal metrics.

*Set a goal to reach the ideal metric that defines success and fail-
ure.* In basketball, you have a rim with a net hanging from it,
attached to a backboard at the end of a well-defined court. You
have a limited four quarters to put the ball through that hoop
as many times as you can before the final buzzer sounds.

In your own workplace, it pays to have your ideal metrics
equally well defined. What are you going to do? To what specifications? Where? How fast? How often? How accurate? At what
cost? How much time and money and how many worker hours
can you use to whip things into shape and get the job done?
What happens if you don't get it done?

There's no point in stealing the ball until you learn where
the basket is.

*Track your progress toward the ideal stats and analyze prob-
lems.* Break the work or task into small chunks or steps and look
for patterns. Do you do better with certain coworkers than
others? Do you work better with certain clients than others? Do
projects of certain magnitude cause problems more often than
others? Formulate and test theories about what hinders your
progress. Observe, collect data, think, question. A problem well
defined leads to a problem soon solved.

Act on the truth; don't hide it. You'll generally find the truth hidden between the two often-expressed sports commentators' summations as they look at lopsided game scores and player stats: "Statistics can be misleading" and "Statistics tell the whole story."

A few months ago, my husband dashed into a local supermarket to buy some advertised energy bars. At the appropriate counter he located only one box of a dozen bars—half of the advertised special. He pulled that box off the shelf and called out to a stocker walking by, "Would you help me find another box of these energy bars? Your ad says 'Buy One and Get One Free' and I can find only one box on the shelf."

"Okay." The stocker followed him over to the shelf and looked around a moment. Not finding another box himself, he turned to my husband and said, "Sorry, sir, I can't let you take that box. It's our last one. You can buy only half the bars in the box." He reached for the box, took it out of my husband's hand, and started piling the dozen small single energy bars on the shelf.

"Wait a minute," my husband said. "I want that whole box."

"Sorry, but I can't let you buy it."

"What do you mean—you can't let me buy it?" My husband was growing a little impatient at this point. "Where's the manager?"

"She's over there," the stocker mumbled, picking up the energy bars for safekeeping under his arm. "I'll go ask her."

"Okay." Bewildered at this strange behavior, my husband stood there rather impatiently while the stocker made his way over to the department manager at the end of the aisle. He watched as they had a brief conversation, and the stocker returned to where my husband stood.

"No, she said you couldn't buy them. She'll sell you a few of them, but we have to leave some on the counter for other customers to come in to buy."

"This is crazy." My husband shook his head, stalked out of the store, got in his car, and started to leave. No, this was nonsensical. He'd taken ten minutes of his lunch time to stop in for energy bars and he wasn't about to take no from somebody who didn't have the power to say yes. He walked back inside to the customer-service counter and asked for the store manager, who happened to be outside at the gas aisle settling a problem. "Do you know why you can't sell me a box of energy bars—why you have to save them to sell to the next customer?"

She looked a little puzzled. He briefed her on the details of the previous conversations. Astonished at the tale and with quick apology, she pressed the service button to the inside department manager: "Sell this customer the energy bars!"

The upshot: The department manager knew her stats, and she got dinged on her performance reviews for being out of stock on a sale item. Rather than improving her purchasing system, she attempted to hide the inventory problem.

It's an all-too-common problem and reaction: Deny the problem rather than fix it. Instead, know your stats so you can set your improvement plan.

Raise the bar. Winning teams are made up of winning individuals. They come early. They stay late. They run laps. They shoot baskets. First, as a team, focus on the external competition. Benchmark against the best in your industry to excel as an organization.

Then focus on your personal record. Athletes benchmark their stats with the rest of the players in their league every season.

Movie stars benchmark their box-office draw against other stars currently playing in theaters. Lawyers benchmark their cases won and lost against their counterparts with the same specialties. CEOs benchmark their company's progress during their tenure at the helm against that of other CEOs in similar situations. You, too, can select colleagues among your professional associations to benchmark against.

Then compete against your own record season after season, project after project. Continue to raise the bar so that you stay out in front and set the standard for those you lead. As they say in the game, records are made to be broken.

*D*o you know your stats?

The greatest danger of most of us is not that our aim is too high and we miss it, but that our aim is too low and we reach it. —UNKNOWN

✶ As a Signature Star, Your Autograph Says You . . .
Keep metrics on your performance, and continue to raise the bar.

EIGHTEEN

CALL A HUDDLE

When the competition gains the lead, when a star player fouls out, when a team gets rattled, when tension mounts, the general inclination is to call a huddle and talk things over. What's the problem? What changes do we need to make? Do we need a new strategy? What plays aren't working? What else should we try?

Just the opposite often happens in business. When problems surface and tension mounts, the inclination is to stop talking and hoard information. People crouch behind their computers and send flaming e-mail when forced to communicate. Instead of fixing problems, they try to hide the gaffes from the guy in the next department. Instead of asking for feedback, they fear straightforward discussions with the boss. Instead of brainstorming solutions, they distrust the colleague around the corner to assess a concern fairly.

As managers recount their experiences in the area of communication, they tend to divide people into two camps:

The successful who share information . . .

- "We have a senior project manager who supervises several teams, sits in on many teleconferences, and attends many technology conferences. As soon as he gets back to the office, he'll e-mail a list of summarized items of important information to the rest of his staff who didn't get to attend and other selected people with a note 'just in case you were busy and missed it.' He's very effective with his teams and is well liked."

- "Whatever the boss knows, she passes it on quickly—every morning in a staff meeting with her direct reports. That makes it easy to know what our priorities are for the day, to stay in tune with our customers, and to make any shifts in direction with the executive team."

- "The culture in my former company was 'Try to make your footprint look really small.' But my old boss didn't buy into that. We were the acquired company on several occasions. And he never would 'hide out' in fear like others did. His attitude was, 'We're here—we'd like to work with you, the acquirer, and share our information. We can embrace change.' He was accepted well and respected for that."

And those who hoard it . . .

- "The president of the company eventually died of a heart attack—paranoid of sharing information. Being the only one with all the information put him in total control. He didn't want people to meet without him. It got so bad that people would not speak up at all. It cost the company millions of dollars."

- "We have a guy we call 'The White Knight.' We'll be working on a client project—ten steps. He'll tell the consultants involved only eight of them. Then when they can't get the project to fly, he comes in at the last minute with the missing information and saves the day. He does this repeatedly. He has created huge animosity among the team. . . . Many very good people are looking for another job."

- "We acquired a company from a different industry. The sales manager there had been with the company for many, many years and could have helped us a lot by giving us information such as highlighting top customers to go after and the right products to pitch. We thought it was that kind of information we were buying when we acquired his company. But the sales manager thought if he 'doled it out slowly' to us that we'd need him more. It was just the reverse. We finally gave up and went around him."

- "We had a VP in daily meetings with the rest of the senior executive team who was always in a hurry mode. She got information but would not share it with the people responsible for taking the action. Very frustrating for those staffers. They developed an 'I don't care' attitude. Her attitude seemed to be, 'I'll tell you when it's time to get on it.' She was intimidated by people on her staff who knew more about the technical work than she did. She would call us in one on one to ask questions for her education. Then she'd go back to the senior executive committee to answer their questions—without credit to the staff who provided all the details and analysis. . . . She eventually lost her job."

- "We had a senior engineer who'd never share any of his experience. We'd spend all this effort on a time-consuming engineering study, and when we'd finish the study and report the results, *then* he'd come forward with confrontational information to refute our study—information that he'd had all along. He withheld the information, rather than contribute to the study upfront, just to prove that he was smarter than we younger engineers. It was a habitual attitude of his."

- "I'm a member of a large religious organization, where the leader's a great motivator and visionary. But he's made it clear that everyone else is only an implementer—that he has all the ideas and information. That organization's gonna die sooner or later."

As you may have guessed, the group who guards information seems to be larger than the group who shares it. That ratio correlates to the ratio of those who succeed as leaders in an organization and those who don't.

Corporate "siloing" has become a cliché because the habit is blossoming into a full-blown blight on our business culture. According to a recent survey from the American Management Association of 493 U.S. and international executive members and customers, 83 percent reported that silos exist in their organizations. Respondents attributed the silos to the typical reasons that you probably experience in your own area of the world: turf wars and territorial management (83 percent), lack of cooperation (72 percent), power struggles (60 percent), personality conflicts (56 percent), lack of accessibility (35 percent), poor response on deadlines (34 percent).[1]

With numbers like these, is it any wonder that cross-functional work gets done at all? If you pick up the phone and call another department with information—any information—

chances are, you're well on your way to becoming a hero just
for responding.

Those who share information demonstrate . . .

- Leadership qualities
- Big-picture thinking
- Teamwork
- Self-confidence
- Maturity
- Common sense

Those who hoard information demonstrate . . .

- Territorialism
- Limited vision
- Poor self-management and organizational skills
- Pettiness and insecurities

In addition to your willingness to share information, the
power of communicating *well* what you know to those who want
to know marks you individually as a Signature Star. In his autobiography *Jack: Straight from the Gut*, Jack Welch, former CEO of
General Electric, writes about the power of communication skills
of one of his subordinates. "I passed over Tom for the job and
brought in an outsider who had once run GE's silicone operations. As a young manager in the plastics business in the early
1960s, I was blown away by the presentations he gave at division-
wide meetings. He was the most articulate of all the leadership.
His speaking skills were particularly impressive to me."[2]

Sharing information is as critical to your business as passing the ball is in a basketball game. Calling a huddle will rejuvenate your team and ultimately determine your success or failure on the court.

*D*o you have a reputation for being the catalyst in bringing people together to share information freely? How effective are your presentation skills when you have the floor?

Communication is a measurable asset.   —SUSAN SAMPSELL

✴ **As a Signature Star, Your Autograph Says You . . .**
Share information rather than hoard it.

PART FOUR

KEEP YOUR FOCUS

$\mathcal{Y}$ou don't have to be around sports long to understand the importance of focus. Just turn on a televised game and you'll hear these comments:

- "They must control the tempo of the game."
- "They should stick to the fundamentals."
- "They need to keep their heads in this ballgame."
- "They've scratched and clawed their way back into this game."
- "They have to crank it up."
- "They must capitalize on their opportunities."
- "They have to pull out all the stops."
- "They gave us a wake-up call."
- "We knew what we had to do, and we went out and did it."
- "We need to take one game at a time."
- "It's do or die."

Focus can mean the difference between going home the winner or going home the loser. At work the mandate is equally clear. Focus leads to the best decisions, proper priorities, appropriate timing, powerful momentum, and remarkable results.

NINETEEN

KEEP YOUR EYE ON THE BALL

Have you ever watched a complacent team fall apart when an opponent suddenly closes the gap on a substantial lead? They begin to throw sloppy passes that get intercepted. It's as if they're tossing bricks toward the backboard. They fail to rebound. Defenders leave the center wide open. They foul the opponents in a 2-1 free-throw situation. In short, they experience a major meltdown.

Fans start to yell, "Calm down!" "Get your head in the game." "Keep your eye on the ball." If the team doesn't heed the warnings, they'll likely lose the game.

They start a good game—they just fail to finish it for lack of focus.

Jerry West knows a thing or two about focus. For the past three decades, he has been responsible for keeping the Los Angeles Lakers laced with top talent. Now, he's moved on to make over the Memphis Grizzlies franchise. Some have called him the dean of NBA talent executives. No one would argue about his clarity of focus. Sportswriter Roland Lazenby describes a particular day almost twelve years ago when he walked in on Jerry at a Lakers' training-camp session at Klum Gym at the University of Hawaii:

I walked in and was stunned to see him out on the floor, shooting the basketball, delivering one perfect 16-footer after another. The ball would settle through the net and hit the floor with just enough spin to send it right back to the shooter. West hardly had to move to retrieve it. Then he started the process over. He studied the goal, and this was the most unsettling thing.

I later figured Jerry West had sighted the goal probably no fewer that two million times since his grade-school days, when he first began lofting a ball at a hoop suspended above the dirt outside his West Virginia home. And here he was, some forty years later, pausing, studying again, as if he was seeing something for the first time, discovering something that the rest of us couldn't see. That had always been the hallmark of West's ability as a player and a team executive, the ability to see things that others couldn't see. Still, I was puzzled that day why he paused so long between shots, staring at the goal. So when he came off the floor, I asked why he had spent so much time studying.

"Because every goal is different," he said. "You have to look at each one of them and figure it out."[1]

Focus is not a new mantra, but the word is getting broad play today because we live and work at such a fast pace. We often feel like captive passengers looking out the window on a runaway train. So much competes for our attention in the wave of technology and around-the-clock media coverage that we don't know *where* to focus. The temptation to scatter our attention tantalizes us to try too many things at once. And the temptation teases even those at the top with the biggest pocketbooks.

That's why you see telecommunication companies buying entertainment producers, airline companies buying record companies, and auto manufacturers buying satellite TV systems.

That also explains why individual managers scramble to staff a new customer-service center in February and dismantle it in July. That's why you see someone go back to school for an MBA in September and then drop out and move across country to take a sales position in October. That's why you see vice presidents hire fourteen new managers the first quarter of the year, lay them off the next quarter, and then hire them back as consultants the following quarter.

The zigzag in direction doubles the time and effort it takes people and organizations to reach their goals:

Lack of focus depletes your energy. Verify the data yourself: Have you noticed that the days you go home from work the most exhausted are the days when you feel as though you started a thousand projects and finished none? Incomplete tasks leave you feeling wasted.

Signature Stars focus and finish. Average performers get sidetracked by everything that comes along, often under the banner of "multitasking." Multitasking comes highly overrated and can be deceptive. The sum total of your attention is actually decreased when you multitask. Multitasking is just rapid attention switching. And every time you switch focus from one project or issue to another, you're losing some of your energy and concentration.

Lack of focus decreases your impact. A few Saturdays ago, my to-do list seemed particularly stressful. Every item on the list is

something I enjoy doing—but I simply couldn't figure out how to
fit into the day's schedule:

- Continue interviewing people for my book
- See granddaughter play soccer
- Finish making new placemats
- Have guests over for dinner who want our advice on a
  business deal
- Cook dinner and take it to my parents (after my mom's
  surgery)
- Exchange damaged item at the mall before time limit
  expires (Okay, so I didn't enjoy this errand—I just needed
  the item)

Well, you guessed it—I tried to get them all in (except for the
mall exchange), and the impact was insignificant. The two book
interviews were rushed. I had no time to spend with my granddaughter before or after the game. I failed to finish all the
placemats so I still couldn't use them. We met the friends at
a restaurant. The dinner delivered to my parents was a pop-in
and pop-out affair, when I would have enjoyed visiting longer.
Low or no impact anywhere.

It's true on a personal level. It's true at work. Scattered effort
leads to scattered results.

> It is better to excel in any single art than to arrive only at
> mediocrity in several.   —PLINY THE YOUNGER (A.D. 61–ca. 113)

Generally, these things break our concentration and focus: the
dim lights of the goal, tweaking the intriguing, and poor time
management.

The Dim Lights of the Goal

We have misaligned our priorities. (We talked about this in the previous chapter.)

Tweaking the Intriguing

A project that's fun, interesting, or visible creates more passion in us, so it's easy to fiddle with those set projects to the neglect of what's most important.

Poor Time Management

These are some of the major culprits:

- *Doing a subordinate's job for them rather than teaching them how to do it.* Operating a communication training firm, I hear this productivity issue surface over and over with senior executives: "My people can't write. Every month I get these same reports from my division directors, and I spend hours and hours reading them and rereading them, trying to figure out what's important and what's not. Then I have to extract the key elements and put them in my general report to the executive leadership team. I wish these people would learn how to write a good executive summary." But why should they when the boss is doing their job for them every month?
- *Repeating delegated tasks—again, and again, and again.* The staff soon learns that you don't really intend for them to do the project until you explain it the fifth time. It's like saying to your kids, "Pick up your toys—this is the last time I'm going to tell you this is the last time."
- *Planning by the seat of the pants.* Crises resulting from lack of forethought cripple current opportunities.

- *Waiting.* Rarely do all the facts ever come in. If you're waiting for approvals, set up systems to operate with as few approvals as necessary. Keep as close to the coach as possible to listen for new plays, and then execute based on the update.

Even in the middle of difficult personal situations, focus can be your secret weapon in coping successfully. Mike Duffy, president of Corporate Television Network, explains how he kept his focus at work during the tragic death of his teenage daughter and his father: "I focus on what kind of person I *want* to be. Through it all, despite my feelings, I tried to focus on what kind of person I *wanted* to be—how I *wanted* to respond to the circumstances."

Focus involves your will—and your won't. Decide what you won't let waylay you. Focus on your priority. Focus on the present.

One thing completed is worth ten things "on hold." Only when you drop the ball through the hoop does the score go on the board. Only when you finish negotiating the contract do you get the bonus. Only when you finish the marketing study can you design the best advertising and publicity campaign. Only when you finish collecting the data can you write the feasibility report. Consider redesigning your work so that you get a sense of satisfaction that comes from finishing something—completely.

Focus and finish so the score goes on the board.

*W*hat is fracturing your focus?

Genius is nothing but a power of sustained attention.

—WILLIAM JAMES

✶ **As a Signature Star, Your Autograph Says You . . .**
Focus.

TWENTY

FOCUS ON THE FUNDAMENTALS

Have you ever seen a championship team that couldn't pass, dribble, rebound, ace their free throws, and sink their jump shots inside the paint? If they don't have the basics perfected, they're not likely to progress to the play-offs. It sounds like a foundational principle—that the basics come before the championship banners.

Yet people often try the opposite at work. For example, in my field of publishing, meeting planners at professional conferences always schedule sessions on the fundamentals for beginning writers, sessions such as writing dialogue, constructing plots, or developing nonfiction proposals. Which sessions do most beginners attend? Sessions on finding an agent, negotiating a contract, or generating publicity. Do you see a problem here? They've skipped the fundamental step of getting the book written! They go for the glitz and glamour rather than the grinding work. Conference planners are repeatedly baffled by this registration rationale.

Big successes, in most any endeavor, are built from all the basics stacked end to end.

Allen Bechtel, a regional claims manager for a midsize insurance company, talks about doing the basics right—staying in touch with your clients and reminding them of the value of the service you provide: "Many corporations self-insure. Even so, we tried to tell our agents how important it was to report to them the status on small claims and let them know about their exposures. We'd tell our agents to diary their files and report again to the clients in thirty days. But many of the agents would ignore that—until the customers called to complain. Our agents just didn't see the importance of it. But when our agents started to see the difference this one little check-back made, our volume went up dramatically. They saw a huge benefit."

Never let well enough alone.   —DR. JOYCE BROTHERS

On the other hand, a former business owner and CEO talks about a new company owner doing the basic things wrong— spending money frivolously: "He forgot our core business and some of the basics of running a business. He let ego drive his decisions. He felt he was in a race with a competitor to acquire more companies. And he made decisions to buy companies and other things that would appeal to the analysts on Wall Street— but be bad for our business ultimately. Like buying a company jet to fly his wife to Amelia Island for dinner. We just needed the money for other things. He quickly drove a very profitable business into Chapter 11."

Taking every shot from center court may not be the fastest way to the play-offs. While the few that drop through the hoop will garner wild applause, the ones that miss will cost you the game.

> *I don't know that there are any shortcuts to doing*
> *a good job.*   —JUSTICE SANDRA DAY O'CONNOR

In your work decisions, consider the total investment of time and dollars and the cost of poor quality and damaged reputation. Pass. Dribble. Rebound. Excel at your free throws and jump shots. Perfect the basics if you intend to win the championship title.

What fundamentals have you forgotten?

_____

> *The ability to prepare to win is as important as the*
> *will to win.*   —BOBBY KNIGHT

_____

✶ As a Signature Star, Your Autograph Says You . . .
Excel at the fundamentals.

TWENTY-ONE

DON'T DOUBLE DRIBBLE

Double dribbling falls into the category of what some sports commentators call "mental mistakes"—those senseless errors made not for lack of skill or because of pressure from the opponent but because of inattention.

Mental mistakes happen in a world of complexity. Even our pastimes are complex. Take shopping for example. I had just finished selecting drapery rods and the sales associate totaled the purchase at $383.

"Great," I said. "I'd like to use these coupon certificates worth $350 against this purchase, and I'll put the remainder on my charge card."

"No problem," the sales associate said. "But I'll need to call the warehouse and ask them to write up a separate ticket for the rod that we were out of stock on, which they'll ship directly from there. I'll get them on the phone, and you can give them your contact information, charge-card number, and mailing address for the shipment while I process the rest of your order. Since you're using these award coupons, I have to write each coupon

119

number on the receipts and then staple them together. So it's
going to take awhile to ring this transaction up."

I can't say she didn't warn me. But I took the phone and she
got on the register, and we squared away that transaction in
about twenty minutes.

"Now, one more thing," I said, before walking away. "I need
a refund on this curtain rod I bought in here last week that
doesn't fit my window—it was $16."

"I'm sorry, but I can't handle refunds here in Draperies. You'll
need to go to Customer Service at the front of the store."

"Where there's the long line?" I protested. "I've already been
in this department two hours, finding what I need."

"I don't think it's too long this time of day." She smiled
apologetically.

I trudged to the front of the store to discover she was right.
The customer-service agent asked if she could help.

"I need to get a refund on this curtain rod. Here's the receipt."

"You'll need to take that to Draperies," the agent said.

"I've just been in Draperies, and Kristin said they don't do
refunds there—that I needed to bring it here to you."

"Of course they do refunds. You must have talked to somebody who doesn't know. Just a minute." She picked up the
phone; Draperies placed her on hold. We waited. Two minutes.
Five minutes. Ten minutes.

"Look, other people are walking up to get refunds at your
counter—why can't you give me a refund on a curtain rod?"
I protested. I considered just walking out at this point because
the transaction had already cost a bundle of time. But we were
into the principle of the thing.

"Because a drapery purchase is different." Someone came

on the phone line hanging at her ear, and they had a brief conversation. Then she turned her attention back to me. "Kristin says she's by herself, and she just got busy with another customer. You can come on back there to her department, and she'll help you with the refund when she finishes, but it may be awhile."

"May I speak to a manager, then."

She called the manager over, and I explained the situation. "I've just spent $17,000 on carpet from your store and received $350 in award coupons because of that purchase. So I came in to buy some drapery rods with those coupons. You were out of stock on one of the drapery rods in this store and we had to order from the warehouse. I spent twenty minutes with them, placing that order. Now, all I want is a $16 refund for this curtain rod, and I've been standing here at Customer Service for twenty minutes waiting and I can't seem to get the refund."

"I'm sorry. Let me see what the problem is."

I thought I had just told her. But the customer-service agent summarized the issues again: (1) Drapery purchases typically can be refunded only from that department. (2) That department is understaffed. (3) Customer Service could act as a backup—except that the rod was included on a receipt against which an award coupon was charged. (4) Other purchases total more than the amount of the award coupons—but those "don't count" because they are being billed to the warehouse, which is shipping the out-of-stock rod.

The store manager seemed totally baffled about how to handle the dilemma.

"Can you simply reach into your register and just hand me the $16 cash?" I suggested.

She thought it over. I had now been in the store close to three hours. Finally, she said, "I guess so—and then I'll straighten it all out later." Pity the poor store associate assigned to simplify that store's refund procedure—if the manager decided to untangle the mess permanently.

In other work situations, we have layer upon layer of similar complexity: data to collect and report to level one, level-one data to be rolled up to level-two supervisors and combined, level-two reports to be combined and rolled up to level-three supervisors and so forth, reports to analyze and accept or reject, meetings to review and discuss issues, approvals to take action, paperwork to document what we've done.

"We've always done it that way," "There must be a reason— they were doing it long before I came on the scene," "This is what I find in the file," and "That's the way they want it done" are insufficient reasons to continue in outdated complexities. Our consultants battle this bulge of obstinacy frequently as we iden- tify boilerplate documents and formats that have long outlived their usefulness in our client organizations. The conversation typically goes like this:

Booher consultant: "This report doesn't say anything new. All the information is available elsewhere. I think you could eliminate it."

"That may be premature. I think they still want it," the report author responds.

"Who is 'they'?"

"Wherever these reports end up. We send them to the regional vice president."

"I've spoken to the regional vice president, and she says this information is redundant to what she already has."

"But other people are on the copy list. They extract information from it too."

"Are you sure they need it?"

"We've been sending it to them ever since John took over in that department."

"What do they use it for?"

"They pull out some of the data, I think."

"Could you just send them the data—without writing the long report?"

"This is the way they want it."

The Booher consultant talks to the people reading the report in John's department: "What do you do with the X report when you receive it?"

"We either toss it or file it. We generally have already seen the information in an e-mail that comes in on the 10th."

"So why does that group continue to compile that report?"

"They have to compile it anyway for their regional vice president."

And so it goes. The complexity remains until someone takes the responsibility of simplifying it.

> *This is the age in which one cannot find common sense*
> *without a search warrant.*   —GEORGE F. WILL

Ask questions about what you do and why you do it. You can do the honors yourself or pay a consultant big bucks to do it for you. According to Peter Drucker, that's his key role as an outsider: "My greatest strength as a consultant is to be ignorant and ask a few questions." Outside eyes and ears have two advantages: (1) You're forced to break things down simply to make

them understandable. (2) You're forced to be honest, to tell it
like it is. Why you do what you do has to make logical sense.
If it doesn't, you'll be challenged to change it.

For example, I recently worked with a client who kept telling
me that they provided quality service. My question to them:
"What do you mean by 'quality service'?"

The sales manager responded, "We provide exceptional sales-
support service to our distributors."

I tried again, "Such as what kind of service exactly? What
kind of service do you provide that other reps calling on the
same distributors don't provide?"

"Customer service when they sell into the large accounts," the
sales manager responded, as if I were a little dense. Yet I knew if
he couldn't articulate to me in a simple way what the benefits of
their customer-support sales service was, it was highly unlikely
their account reps would be able to state these benefits in their
sales presentations to distributors.

"But specifically I need a definition of what you mean when
you call on your distributors and tell them that if they offer your
products to their customers, you will provide them exceptional
service. What do you mean by 'exceptional service'?"

"Well, . . . just the typical customer-service things."

"So you don't really do anything that your competitors don't
offer?" I clarified.

"Not really. Our competitors all have a fast turnaround
time—they ship within seven to ten days. They have online order-
ing, so it's easy and fast. Their products are well made also."

I repeated my question. "So what do you mean by 'exceptional customer service'?"

"Well, we don't have all these extra setup charges when they

order. So that makes it a lot easier. That's really the big difference. When you factor that in, it makes taking the order a lot
easier and faster."

Finally, we had arrived at the simple meaning of "exceptional customer service" written all over their sales literature—
their differentiation in the marketplace. With this simple
information, we restructured their sales presentations and their
approach accordingly. He walked away with simple language
that his customers could understand.

With the same information—what you do and why you do
it—you can begin to simplify and increase your own impact and
results. It's a common trap to think your customers are the
culprits in demanding complexity.

Occasionally, we at our own company trip ourselves up
by making things harder than they have to be. Case in point:
Part of our uniqueness in our training programs at Booher
Consultants is that we offer customization. Although we prefer
to conduct our standard off-the-shelf programs, some clients
like to send us their own documents to incorporate into our
business and technical writing courses particularly.

With one such client, the liaison was dragging his feet
in forwarding the sample documents to us in time to incorporate them into the curriculum before the scheduled work-
shop. The account executive reminded, cajoled, and pleaded,
but the samples did not arrive. The trainer was in a dither
to analyze the new documents and turn them into exercises.
The production manager was in a dither to produce the special-
ized manuals. The coordinator was in a dither to ship the
materials.

Finally, the account executive left a message with the client along these lines: "Send us the samples or else." That prompted a callback from the client liaison: "Why are you wanting to customize this course? We'd rather use Booher generic exercises—our documents are confidential." Less work for us. We were delighted. They were delighted. Simple.

Ask questions. Don't assume complexity is a necessity.

> *Everything should be made as simple as possible,*
> *but not one bit simpler.*   —ALBERT EINSTEIN

Chase the paper trail and shorten it. Identify all the routine pieces of paper and electronic documents that come into and leave your office—reports, e-mail, forms, and so forth—and map their trail. Where do they come from and where are they going when they leave your office? Why? You may be shocked at the unnecessary steps in your processes that create extra work for everybody in the path.

Eliminate the mental mistakes. Look for the mistakes caused by inattention rather than errors in judgment or lack of skill. A $1.6 billion media company in a niche market involving satellite broadcasts discovered they were failing to renew on average 72 percent of their corporate subscribers from year to year in one particular region. Further investigation pinpointed the cause to be customer dissatisfaction over "mental mistakes": Failure to ship the workbooks for its educational sessions. Failure to ship the brochures containing the programming schedule to the corporate headquarters so audiences knew when the broadcasts aired. Failure to send backup videotapes of a broadcast when the satellite was down due to inclement weather.

In other words, customers had no complaints about the

programming, the price, the policies, or the technology. The dissatisfaction stemmed from the mental mistakes—things the staff failed to do to complete the service. When this region corrected these mental mistakes, their annual subscriber renewals skyrocketed.

Simplify things—words, documents, data collection, reporting, review and approval processes, meeting agendas, partnership agreements, organizational structure—so you can discover and eliminate the unnecessary. Here's a key question to ask yourself: Would this work get done just as well if I didn't take this step? If so, skip it.

If you can pass the ball in bounds and then shoot a basket, why run and dribble at all?

What processes do you need to simplify or eliminate?

_____

> *The secret of all power is—save your force. If you want high pressure you must choke off waste.* —JOSEPH FARRELL

_____

✷ As a Signature Star, Your Autograph Says You . . .
Simplify things, and eliminate the unnecessary.

TWENTY-TWO

SLOW THE TEMPO

If you've ever seen a basketball game turn into a track meet, then you know that players get rattled and sometimes make snap decisions. They pass to a teammate who's covered. They charge into the lane where there's no opening and have the ball stolen. They take a jump shot when they're off balance.

Impatience can cost you the game. It can also cost you a client, your job, your reputation, your business, your life savings, or your family.

Speed has become a criteria for quality in many quarters, and there's growing pressure to make a fast decision—any decision—just to keep the plates spinning at work. On occasion, it takes courage to slow the tempo enough to follow the principles in Proverbs for sound decision-making.

> *Our most important decisions are made while we are*
> *thinking about something else.* —MASON COOLEY

Slow the tempo until you can get the facts. Proverbs says, "Everyone with good sense wants to learn."[1] No, the facts don't speak for themselves. They need interpretation. But facts make things clearer than no facts at all.

Slow the tempo until you're sure your mind is open to new ideas. Have you ever worked with someone who started with the premise, "The answer is no; now what's the question?" They probably haven't won many promotions for leadership or innovation. Again, Proverbs nails it: "He who answers before listening—that is his folly and his shame."[2]

Slow the tempo until you study both sides of an issue. According to Proverbs: "The first to present his case seems right, till another comes forward and questions him."[3] If you've sat through many budget meetings at work, you understand the truth of this Proverb. Everyone can justify their recommendations and requests for funds—until you hear other knowledgeable people in the group begin to question the requester on the budget specifics. Just about any proposal sounds good until you hear from those against it.

> *Keep cool and you command everybody.*
>
> —LOUIS DE SAINT JUST

The city where I live recently mailed out a sample ballot of twenty-two propositions up for a vote in our state elections. I studied the issues, marked my sample ballot, and took it to the polls with me as a reference tool. When I signed in, the election official held two ballots toward me and asked me if I wanted to vote in the state election or both the state and the city elections.

"I didn't know there was a city election."

"We didn't mail out a sample ballot," she said. "There's just one proposed amendment on the city ballot."

"What is that?"

"That proposition is to continue the tax that funds the agency that keeps the city's crime rate so low—to keep drug traffic down, to keep our kids safe, to protect our businesses, to keep the streets and the shopping malls free of gangs. That sort of thing. Do you want a ballot?"

Any guess which way she was voting? Either side of an issue, proposal, recommendation, or business plan sounds right until you hear the other viewpoint. That's why Proverbs suggests there's wisdom in getting input from many people: "With many counselors there is safety."[4] The more people you hear from on an issue, the more likely you'll hear all sides.

That's not to say, of course, that you should call a meeting every time you want to reset the cafeteria clock. Decisive people may sometimes resist getting input from others for several reasons: (1) They think it wastes time. (2) They feel as if they're shirking their own responsibility. (3) They fear they may lose control of the decision or situation.

Collaborative decision making doesn't mean consensus necessarily. You have choices. You can ask advisers—staff, clients, peers, outsiders, family—for their input individually. Or you can call together your team—those with a direct interest in the outcome of a decision—and ask for their input while letting them know you yourself will be making the final decision. Even if they don't have the chance to make the final decision, they'll appreciate being involved in the process and having their opinions considered. In all these cases, you have the benefit of input and multiple viewpoints on your issue.

What you always do before you make a decision is consult.
The best public policy is made when you are listening to

*people who are going to be impacted. Then, once a policy
is determined, you call on them to help you sell it.*

—ELIZABETH DOLE

Slow the tempo until you've asked God for wisdom. Fortunately
for us, God never tires of our asking. "If you need wisdom—if you
want to know what God wants you to do—ask him, and he will
gladly tell you. He will not resent your asking."[5] A major condition of our receiving wisdom, however, is our commitment to use
it—to do what God tells us to do. Proverbs says, "Seek his will in
all you do, and he will direct your paths."[6]

Consider the bad decisions that have dented your past. How
many of them did you make before you had the appropriate
facts? How many of them did you make against other people's
advice—or without any advice? In how many of the situations did
you have a preconceived idea about what you should do before
you analyzed the issue? In how many of the situations did you
become impatient and act before getting clear direction from
God?

Case closed.

When the pace around you picks up, know when to hold onto
the ball and take your time.

A re you letting false or self-imposed deadlines dictate important decisions?

Act quickly, think slowly.   —GREEK PROVERB

✴ **As a Signature Star, Your Autograph Says You . . .**

Know when to take your time in making sound decisions.

TWENTY-THREE

MAKE THE FAST BREAK

Defensive players focus on blocking, rebounding, or stealing the ball. As soon as they get their hands on the ball, they automatically look for opportunities to either make a fast break for the goal or lob a pass to a teammate already downcourt under the goal and ready to lay it in the basket before the opponent knows what's happened. Intercepting a pass, then calling a time-out to wait for the opponents to regroup themselves would be ludicrous.

Yet that's the impact of indecisiveness in the workplace. Opportunities pop up, people get excited about them, they make recommendations—and then they wait. And wait. And wait. The opportunity passes. The decision is made by default.

Sometimes the indecisiveness is on our own part. Decisions produce doubt and sleepless nights. "Should I?" or "Shouldn't I?" questions slosh around like waves that leave us unsettled, unsure, unfocused.

But it doesn't have to be that way. These two guiding principles can help you know when to risk a fast break for the basket.

Make a fast break on a moral issue. In the Bible, there's the story of Joseph in the top post of authority in running the king's household. While Joseph went about his work in the palace, Potiphar's wife continued to let him know she had far more interest in him personally than as an employee. He kept his distance as much as possible, but one day, she grabbed his clothes and made a pass that couldn't be ignored. Joseph fled, leaving her irate; he didn't even stay around a few minutes to think about it or talk it over "to keep from hurting her feelings."[1]

When it comes to moral choices, fast is good. We all have to make daily decisions about obedience to our moral compass and God's laws. Not to decide is to decide. Tentativeness on moral decisions leaves you open for attack, for second thoughts.

Make a fast break when you hear God's clear, strong direction and the path does not contradict foundational biblical principles. Elizabeth Smart was held for nine months by Brian Mitchell and Wanda Eileen Barzee, homeless people excommunicated by the Mormon church, who told friends that God told them to take Elizabeth. Deanna LaJune Laney beat to death her eight- and six-year-old sons and left her fourteem-month-old son alive but severely beaten, saying God told her to do it.[2]

God gets "credited" for a lot of things he never told anybody to do: kidnap kids, murder marriage partners, bomb buildings and innocent victims, conduct illicit sexual affairs, steal trade secrets, or gossip about the gambling habits of the boss. People who say they are doing such under God's direction are badly mistaken.

Even sane, law-abiding businesspeople become confused occasionally when trying to make a quick decision. Here's a solid test on the soundness of your decision: Does what you feel God

leading you to do contradict other foundational biblical principles—principles about money, love, brotherhood, obedience,
integrity, giving, marriage, family responsibilities, or the Ten
Commandments? If so, the direction is not from God.

On the other hand, when you've asked for God's wisdom,
when the decision does not contradict Scripture, and when you
sense a strong direction, go with your gut—whether or not it
makes logical sense. The Bible gives several incidences of Jesus
calling his disciples and expecting them to make an immediate
decision: Peter, Andrew, James, and John all left their fishing
boats immediately when their opportunity came.[3] Matthew,
the tax-collector, did the same when Jesus called him away from
his tax collection booth.[4] Don't you imagine their friends and
coworkers thought them a little irrational and impulsive?

Ken Harbin, former vice president and general manager of
operations for Hunt Oil in Yemen, recalls such a strong direction from God on what at the time seemed like a minor decision
and project. They were in the process of installing satellite
phones in their offices. The workmen had completed most of
the installations except for two key items to make the system
operational. The foreman came to him at the end of the normal
workday and said, "I'll come back in the morning and finish it."

"No. Finish it now. Tonight." Ken insisted, without really
knowing why he was making that unusual decision.

A civil war broke out in the country later that night. Except
for the U.S. embassy, which had its own satellite, theirs was the
only phone in the country for six weeks. The German and the
French embassies had to use the phones in the offices of Hunt
Oil for the next two weeks. That installed phone system enabled
Hunt employees to call their families back in the States to let

them know they were alive and well. Ken credits that decision—not logical and outside the norm—to God's strong direction.

Our unrest frequently results when we confuse God's direction with our own desires. How do you know the difference? Back to the previous chapter: Gather the facts. Keep an open mind. Hear all sides of a situation.

Sound decision-making can be fast or slow. Only you know what is driving your decisions—the deliberation, the deals, the deadlines, or God's direction. If you've prayed for wisdom, feel strong direction, and then refuse to act, that's disobedience. Good things happen to those willing to go with their gut at God's direction.

*H*ave you missed opportunities God has put in your path for lack of courage to make the fast break toward the goal?

A wise man will make more opportunities than he finds.

—FRANCIS BACON

✳ As a Signature Star, Your Autograph Says You . . .
Know when to decide quickly.

TWENTY-FOUR

USE YOUR TIME-OUTS
STRATEGICALLY

The trailing team starts to close the gap, and the tempo of the game speeds up. But no one wants to mention what's happening for fear of stopping the momentum. Your team drops in another basket, then steals the ball, makes a fast break toward the goal, and lays up another two points. The gap closes to six points.

The pace picks up. The opponents dribble downcourt. Your team intercepts a pass and scores again. The gap closes to four points.

The tempo speeds up. The opponent tosses the ball into play again, and as his teammate starts to dribble downcourt, the ball takes a nasty bounce off his foot and sails out of bounds. Your team has the ball again under your own goal.

The pace picks up. Your player gets fouled and makes the free throws. The gap closes to two points.

Which coach is more likely to call a time-out at this point— the gaining team or the leading team? Absolutely correct: the leading team. No coach worth his paycheck would stop that trailing team on the move.

Yet people commit such blunders every day at work with their own teams and projects. They stop progress at the most inopportune times—just before completion and success—by diverting attention to tangential projects or allowing interruptions to take them off course. This practice is as dangerous on the job as on the basketball court.

Build momentum. In his business best seller *The Tipping Point*, Malcolm Gladwell writes about the power of momentum in terms of contagious diseases and epidemics, a concept we readily understand. He says ideas, products, messages, behaviors, and reputations spread just like viruses do. He cites the fall of New York's crime rate and the popularity of various products such as Hush Puppies as textbook examples of epidemics in action. These are clear cases of contagious behavior—just like measles moving through a grade school or neighborhood.

You've probably experienced this phenomenon yourself. No one in your neighborhood is wearing spiked hair. Then almost overnight, everywhere you go, you see people wearing spiked hairdos. Nobody places a radio ad and says, "On June 16, let's all start wearing spiked hair—it's cool." It just spreads like the flu.

You may have experienced this phenomenon at work. Let's say you've been a member of a group that just doesn't seem "to click." There's no camaraderie. Everyone has their own agenda, no shared interests, no particular congeniality. You work through a few projects. Then all of a sudden, the chemistry changes. Almost overnight, you click as a team. Looking back, you don't know when you passed the tipping point, but it happened.

Gladwell's research turned up three important characteristics of this phenomenon: (1) It's contagious—it affects everyone. (2) Little causes have big effects. (3) Change happens not gradually but at one dramatic moment, which he labeled "the tipping point." This last characteristic, the dramatic moment, he insists, is the most important of all because it is the principle that makes sense of the first two.

Closely related to the concept of the tipping point is the power of momentum. Although not necessarily at one dramatic moment, change builds gradually to a powerful result. For example, a salesperson calls or sends a direct-mail piece to a prospect, and the prospect never responds because he has never heard of the salesperson's organization. The salesperson mails and calls. Calls and mails. E-mails and calls. Mails and calls. No response. All of a sudden, the prospect calls the salesperson "out of the blue" and says, "I'm in the market for a widget, and I've heard a lot about your organization." The salesperson responds, "Oh really? Where?" The prospect says, "I don't know specifically. I just see your name everywhere." A closed sale.

Movie stars and pop artists experience the power of momentum through more and longer media exposure. They build momentum for years, perfecting their craft with minor roles and performances in out-of-the-way venues. Then their popularity builds until everybody buys their newest CD or turns up at the box office, making them the talk of the town. The media then refers to them as "overnight successes," unaware of the start of the momentum roll.

Kelsey Grammer serves as another good example of the power of momentum. He started with a six-episode contract on *Cheers,* became a regular, then ended with his own spin-off, *Frasier,* topping off more than a twenty-year television stint. As of the last contract negotiations, Grammer was reportedly the highest paid actor on TV, at $1.6 million per episode. Three Emmys top off his list of achievements and momentum.

Momentum builds even behind an idea. Consider the recent run of no-stars, low-cost TV programming that began with game shows like *Who Wants to Be a Millionaire?* and evolved into what's now known as "reality TV"—everything from survivors, to bachelors selecting marriage partners, to moms redecorating houses, to psychologists soothing psyches.

The power of momentum applies with almost any idea, product, project, or person: It's contagious. A little step forward can have a big impact. Change can be sudden and dramatic.

Employees and organizations experience this same momentum. New products become hugely popular almost overnight. Organizations go from oblivion to household words in a matter of months. Nobody's heard of them; then everybody owns their stock. People build momentum personally. They get on the fast track at work, earning a promotion every few months. Or they lose momentum, turning down a few key assignments or failing to deliver results. Suddenly, they drop off the executive team's radar screen.

Make sure all plays lead to the basket. Your playbook may contain hundreds of diagrams, but they have little value if they don't get the ball and the players to converge on the goal. You can run play after play with absolutely *no* time-outs, but if you don't ever take a shot, you're no closer to winning than if you had no plays at all. All plays and all time-outs have to continually lead you to this one point: getting the ball in the basket.

Jesus understood the power of momentum. He spent the first

thirty years of his life preparing for the last three. And from the time he began his public ministry, his momentum built from obscurity to being worshiped as King. In one three-year build of momentum, he changed the course of history like no one has been able to do before or since. His every action led toward his one goal on earth.

You need similar convergence in your business. Every action you take has to converge in front of the goal. For example, if you're marketing your services as a software-design firm to small businesses, everything you do in your business has to contribute to that goal. Taking out an ad in the small-business journal in your city is a converging play. Attending your local chamber of commerce to meet other small-business owners is a converging play. Mass-mailing a coupon for one-hour's free consulting time to corporations is a nonstrategic time-out. Designing a brochure with a headline that promises to "be the back office for small businesses by writing custom software" is a converging play. Renting office space in a downtown high-rise when your small-business customers never come to you is a nonstrategic time-out.

As you build momentum, don't lose sight of your purpose: getting the ball in the basket.

Don't call time-out when you're open under the basket. When you're on a roll, you want to keep your own team hyped and your opponents confused.

Marketing mavens understand "being on a roll" as they build growing brand awareness with new products. Novelists start a series when they sell a single best seller. Movie producers bring out the sequel when they have a blockbuster at the box office. Snack companies bring out dips to go with their best-selling chips. When shoe manufacturers hit with a popular running shoe, they roll it out in sixteen colors.

Fallen Fortune 500 companies call a time-out under the basket when they dabble in a business they know nothing about or add a new product line before they get the current one established in the market. It's a key reason they slip off the Fortune 500 list.

You call a time-out under the basket when you leave a meeting just before a crucial decision because someone beeped your cell phone to handle an urgent, but unimportant, issue. You call time-out under the basket when you get into a squabble with a team member and have to find a replacement and get them up to speed before the action can resume. You call time-out under the basket when you let a subordinate's project sit on your desk for days or weeks before you add your approval signature.

Limit your time-outs for water. Control needless, time-gobbling interruptions even when you're focused on your goal. Personal disorganization. Do-overs caused by unclear instructions. Trivial voice mails and e-mails that demand a reply. All these things break your concentration on the top priorities for the day. Often one little interruption keeps you from seeing a task through to completion in one sitting.

The momentum of one uninterrupted hour can have huge impact. Give me a day, and I can conquer the world.

Points go on the board when the ball's in play—not during the time-outs. Be the team or the person on the move.

*W*here do you need to build momentum?

If you start to take Vienna—take Vienna.

—NAPOLEON BONAPARTE

✳ **As a Signature Star, Your Autograph Says You . . .**
Understand the power of momentum.

TWENTY-FIVE

TAKE A LOOK-SEE

The power forward dribbles into the lane and, finding herself surrounded by defenders, makes a U-turn and passes back out to the short forward.

Fans shout from the sidelines, "Take your time!" "Look around!" "We're not in a hurry!"

The short forward passes back to the guard. The guard passes back to the forward. The guard bounces it to the center. The center fakes to the left and then bounces it back to the forward, who drives right downtown and lays it in the basket for two points.

What's the difference? A hole in the middle—the timing was perfect.

Business owners can attest to this fact: You can work very hard and still lose everything you have. You do it by driving right up the middle at the wrong time. Executives, managers, and other professionals can attest to this fact: You can work very hard and still lose your job. You do it by driving right up the middle at the wrong time. Sales and marketing people can attest to this fact: You can work very hard and still lose the sale, the client, and the entire market. You do it by driving right up the middle at the wrong time.

IBM knows a thing or two about timing. In fact, they have a reputation in the high-tech industry for permitting smaller companies to run along the bleeding edge and test the market. Then when the market is well established, they move in and dominate. Chalk another one up to their good sense of timing—IBM's purchase of the consulting unit of Pricewaterhouse-Coopers in October 2002. Hewlett-Packard had considered the purchase of the same 30,000-employee PricewaterhouseCoopers consulting unit eighteen months earlier for as much as $18 billion. But the deal was aborted about the time the Internet bubble burst. IBM made the same purchase eighteen months later for $3.5 billion.

A nice savings—or a big loss—depending on your point of view. In any case, timing and context tell the story.

Proverbs warns about charging ahead without considering the timing and the context: "Finish your outdoor work and get your fields ready; after that, build your house."[1] In other words, put first things first. The writer of Ecclesiastes put it more poetically and in great detail: "There is a time for everything, and a season for every activity under heaven: . . . A time to plant and a time to uproot, . . . a time to tear down and a time to build, . . . a time to search and a time to give up, . . . a time to keep and a time to throw away, . . . a time to tear and a time to mend, a time to be silent and a time to speak."[2]

This principle for running a business, managing a corporate division, or planning a project cannot get any clearer than stated in this proverb.

Another modern-day proverb closely paraphrasing the biblical one is this: Don't spend your money before you make it. My city has a large testimony to this principle. A couple built a 16,000-square-foot home that took them three years to complete. They moved in and lived in it only a few months before financial trouble hit that forced them to put it up for sale at $7.2 million and auction off their furnishings. When that didn't bail them out, the mortgage holder repossessed their home.

But we're not just talking literally here—building houses and corporate assets, allocating budgets and bonuses. The issue expands to introducing new products to market, hiring help, opening offices overseas, or changing the charter on charitable contributions.

A school administrator shares the difficulty in discerning a faith issue from a timing issue. At their Christian academy for inner-city youth in Atlanta, the week before school was to start the following Thursday, they had eight children on the waiting list for a lower grade. As an expression of "faith" that God would provide the resources and additional children to fill a class of twenty-four, they made a quick decision to open an additional section to accommodate the eight students on the waiting list, hired a teacher on Monday to begin on Thursday, and ordered all the student materials. Result: The class didn't fill, the additional expense drained cash flow, and the inexperienced teacher struggled all year.

Good intentions, great God, wrong timing.

How do you develop a sense of timing and context? Here are three key questions to quicken that thought process.

Stars travel with the right gear. You never see a winning ball club unload the bus and bustle into the gym without their bag of balls. They never leave it to the host team or the referees to make sure they can start their warm-up drills on time with fully inflated balls. They identify the necessary resources to make things happen.

Do you have the resources you need to get your project off the ground? When King Solomon built his magnificent temple in Jerusalem, notice how he began—with the huge assembly of resources. And that was in addition to the masses of timber and other supplies his father, King David, had already shipped into the country for the project.

As a first step, ask: What resources do I have? Expertise? Credentials? Training? Referrals and network? Money? Staff? What do I still lack and what will it cost to find these things? Identify the resources you'll need before you promise a due date.

Stars don't scrimmage during halftime. The clock runs during halftime, but the players go to the locker room. For starters, they need rest. And second, they don't want the opponents to hear them discuss plays and strategy for the second half. Scrimmaging on the court while the crowd looks on isn't the appropriate time or place for a course correction. They need privacy. In the week that follows, they'll scrimmage and improve for the next game and the next.

The Old Testament prophet Nehemiah had a sense of timing. In talking with his friends, he discovered that his homeland still had security problems, with the walls and gates in need of repair. Although he served in a comfortable and wealthy position in the Persian court, he immediately felt the need to return to his country to lead the rebuilding project.

But he didn't hop on the next plane out. First of all, he fasted and prayed, asking God's leadership to make sure that this was the right thing to do and that he was the right person to do it. When he got the okay there, he still didn't head down to buy his ticket. Next, he stayed on around the palace while waiting until the king noticed his mood and asked the reason for his sadness. Then he told the king and asked permission to go take care of the problem in Jerusalem. And even though the king gave his okay, Nehemiah still didn't dial up a taxi. He lingered a while longer, asking the king for letters of referral that would open a few doors for him along the way. Throughout the story, you'll note that he planned first, traveled second.[3]

Waiting tests our patience. It also tests our maturity. You can do the right things at the wrong time and fail miserably.

Stars create the home-team advantage wherever they are. Have you ever noticed how much effort winning teams put into getting the hometown fans to travel with them to the games on the road? They publish the season's schedule before the first game begins. They sell the best seats to the season-ticket holders. They reserve seats in the stands so supporters can sit together in the visitor's section and sound like a larger group than if seated and shouting as singles around the crowd. They encourage parades to send them off or accompany them to the big games. They arrange welcome-home rallies for the big play-offs and championship games.

Why? Sports teams understand how important setting and support are to success. Context creates connection.

Is the setting right for your projects, goals, and other undertakings? Have you inspired supporters throughout the organization, division, or department to take up your cause?

Notice that when Nehemiah arrived in his homeland, he set out with a few men during the night to organize their venture to rebuild the walls and restore security to the city. But he told no one—not his friends, the religious leaders, or the governing officials—what God had put in his heart to do until the time was right.[4] But once he had his plan in mind, he shared his vision, inspired the people he needed to depend on for help, and together they trusted God to give them success in accomplishing their mission.

The setting and context made the difference. He traveled there to be among them so they could feel the fire in his belly for the project.

Queen Esther had a similar sense of timing. As wife of the Persian king Xerxes, she was in a unique place to ask him to rescind a law that would, in effect, have annihilated her people. But she needed a home-team advantage. Her elderly cousin, Mordecai, who worked around the courtyard, brought her messages. And she asked her maids to pray with her for courage and the right opportunity.

She decided to throw a banquet for the king and tell him how he'd been duped by his right-hand man, Haman, into passing the dangerous edict and then plead for her people. Both the king and Haman show up to her first banquet. But Esther sat tight. When the banquet ended, they went home, knowing nothing more about her plan than that they had an invitation to her second banquet.

So why did Esther not carry out the plan at the first banquet? No one knows for sure, of course. Perhaps it was to let a few more details fall into place. It may have been to catch the king in the right mood. And maybe it was to ensure that she had earned the king's trust and to measure her sphere of influence against Haman's. Whatever the reason, Esther rocked at the second banquet. She revealed Haman's true colors and asked the king to revoke the law. He honored her request, and she saved an entire nation.

She set the context, created the mood, and made her move. The most famous line in her entire story (the book that carries her name in the Old Testament) is this one: "Who knows but that you have come to royal position for such a time as this?"[5] God had a sense of timing to place her there; she had a sense of timing about when to act.

If God has a sense of timing, so should we. Identify your resources, lay your plans, create the home-court advantage, and then wait for the right opportunity. Signature Stars do the right thing at the opportune moment and succeed.

*A*re you applying a full-court press for a good thing at the wrong time?

Don't think there are no crocodiles because the water is calm.
—MALAYAN PROVERB

✶ **As a Signature Star, Your Autograph Says You . . .**
Pay attention to the timing and context.

TWENTY-SIX

DON'T MAKE YOURSELF
PLAY CATCH-UP

The tighter the score, the more intrigued the television viewing audience. With a twelve-point spread, you have time to go to the kitchen for a snack. With an eight-point spread, you can watch the game while you read the newspaper. When the gap closes to two points, the players have your undivided attention.

A runaway ballgame, on the other hand, loses its entertainment value. When your team loses, the crowd snoozes. It's not that coaching couldn't eventually correct the problem. It's not that the players won't learn from their mistakes. It's not that the leading team won't tire at some point. It's just that time runs out. The game ends.

The same thing happens to otherwise successful people and projects. Time runs out too soon. Or, they start too late. Try this self-assessment to see if you might be in danger of getting off to a slow start in your typical game:

- Do you view a typical project as a monumental task, or do you consider it a series of small steps in a longer process?
- Do you find yourself doing unnecessary or easy chores in prime work time?
- Do you frequently postpone tackling tough projects because you feel "too tired"?
- Have you been working on projects so long that they've become stale rather than fresh and exciting?

How you decide to spend your minutes—particularly those upfront minutes—may mean the difference between success and failure on a project. Procrastination is a habit common to most of us at one time or other. We procrastinate when a job seems overwhelming, unpleasant, boring, risky, or unclear. Sometimes procrastination serves as a technique to get others' sympathy or help, to irritate them, or to sabotage their goals.

To sweep your psyche of procrastination, consider these tips and techniques:

- Tease yourself with small, doable chunks or steps.
- Forget perfection and creativity; just start.
- Start on a middle step if the beginning steps have you baffled.
- Mark your place and the next action to be done before you stop work each session.
- Stop and start when things are going well—not when you're stuck. (Otherwise, you'll never want to go back to the task.)
- If you're stuck on a project, give your subconscious time to work out a solution.
- Find a way to make it fun. Involve other people. Make it

a contest. Do it at an odd time. Wear comfortable clothes.
Eat great food. Do it at a relaxing place.

- Make a commitment to someone else to get it done by
  a specific date. Or announce your intentions publicly so
  that loss of face for failure compels you to start and finish.
- Reward any progress at all.
- Start with the most dreaded part so you can get it over with.
  Once you're past that biggest hump, you'll gain energy for
  the rest.

No farmer ever plowed a field by turning it over in his mind.

—UNKNOWN

Piddling can also be a sign of procrastination. Of course,
piddling on purpose is fine. That can be restful. But piddling
when you think you're busy is self-delusion.

Pulling out a win is much easier when you don't have to come
from so far behind.

**What project or decision are you procrastinating about?
Has procrastination cost you a promotion?**

_____

*If you want to make an easy job seem mighty hard, just
keep putting off doing it.*   —OLIN MILLER

_____

✷ As a Signature Star, Your Autograph Says You . . .
Refuse to play catch-up.

TWENTY-SEVEN

LIGHT UP THE SCOREBOARD

TV pregame interviews with the coach can be discouraging.

Sportscaster: "How are things looking for the game today?"

Coach: "We'll be ready. We'd like to have had a couple more days, but we'll be out there."

Sportscaster: "You're referring to the injuries? Mike Frazier's knee twisted in last week's game and Dody's kidney problem?"

Coach: "Right. Dody still won't be in the lineup today. Salinas will be starting in his place."

Sportscaster: "How much action has Salinas seen?"

Coach: "Not as much as we'd have liked. But we've worked with him this week. He's young. Has a lot of energy, passion. He loves the game."

Sportscaster: "Being in your hometown will be a factor, do you think?"

Coach: "That's always a factor."

Sportscaster: "I understand Ted Frankacas has had some

family problems these past few weeks. Missed some practices. Legal troubles trailing him. Can he shake that on the court?"

Coach: "He's dedicated to the game. He's working through those difficulties."

Sportscaster: "And of course on the minds of both teams today, the new change in the rules. Did you agree with that change, and how will it affect the way your team plays today?"

Coach: "One of the stupidest rule changes the NBA has ever come up with. I wholeheartedly disagree. But it's the rule now, and we'll play by it."

Sportscaster: "Well, Coach, we wish you the best out there today."

Coach: "Thanks, Mac."

Even after that gloom and doom, when the game starts, do you think the fans, coach, and owner, will still want a win? Absolutely. Despite short deadlines, absences, untrained players, those with personal problems, and controls and restrictions they disagree with, the fans will still expect results.

Your fans at work demand the same outstanding performance—despite the difficulties. And it is getting more difficult to delight people, no doubt about it. Here's what interviewees have to say about how their life is growing more complex and why it's so difficult to deliver results day after day.

- "The complexity of technology is a big issue—all the time I have to set aside to teach my people what the technology can and should do. Instead, the training people come in here and teach a quick course on how to operate it. What we need is *why* and *when* and *how*. *Why* will this be useful to you? *When* is it appropriate to use this? *How* will it help you do your business better? All this needs to come before the rudimentary rules of how to operate it."

- "Analysis and reporting every week. The 'just-because-it's-possible financial scenarios' syndrome that's infected everyone. I can't get my job done."
- "Travel and the security systems imposed—you're at the mercy of the airlines."
- "I wish all my staff were trained."
- "The immaturity of my support staff and their inability to work as a team—'not my job,' poor attendance records, won't pull their weight."
- "Corporate sending mandates to the field when they are out of the touch with what's going on here."
- "Always going back to school, having to learn and digest new things to stay up to date."
- "My personal life—juggling scheduled activities, household responsibilities, family problems."
- "Conflicting church activities and responsibilities—they never coordinate the activities. You can't have your six-year-old and your twelve-year-old at two different places at the same time—and be at a different location yourself."

Despite the difficulties, our fans keep glancing at the scoreboard, expecting another two points. Three points are even better. How do you deliver consistently without disappointing them?

Reject excuses; face facts. In sales, account executives learn three definitions to enable them to qualify their prospects and spend their time wisely: conditions, concerns, excuses. A condition is a legitimate reason the prospect cannot buy, something over which they have no control or influence. For example, the prospect has no authority or no money or the company's going through a merger and all purchases are frozen. A concern (often called an objection) is a legitimate expression of indecision raised about the product or service. It may be an unresolved condition or a mishandled sales call or failure to show value or create a need. An excuse, on the other hand, is a comment offered to delay or avoid having to disappoint someone with a "no."

What does all this have to do with you if you're not in sales? I'm coming to that in a moment.

Salespeople know a legitimate reason or condition when they hear it. If the prospect says she makes $15,000 a year, they're not likely to sell her a BMW. They don't expect to make the sale, so they spend their time elsewhere. When salespeople hear a legitimate concern or objection, they try to address it. If the prospect says the product won't be delivered in time for his project in San Diego, the salesperson tries to get the delivery date moved earlier. And finally, when salespeople hear an excuse for a no, they know it. They go away and spend their time elsewhere.

> *Some people entertain ideas; others put them to work.*
>
> —UNKNOWN

Treat yourself and your team to the same screening. When you look at your performance individually or as a team, ask yourself these questions:

- Is my performance the result of a legitimate reason, a *condition*—something over which I have no control?
- Is my performance the result of an unresolved *concern*—

a legitimate reason, but something I have some control
over and could change by myself or by working with others
to change?

- Is my performance the result of an *excuse*—a rationalization
about not doing my best and hesitancy to face the truth?

Shareholders, bosses, team leaders, clients, and coworkers
will typically react much like salespeople in the same scenarios.
(1) They understand legitimate reasons and conditions. (2) They
expect you to work to address concerns where you have some
control. (3) They hate excuses and insist that you face the facts.

Shoot for inches. The ball hits the rim and bounces off, or the
ball hits the backboard in the sweet spot and swooshes in. The
difference is inches. The same is true at work: Significant leaps
in work performance do happen; small steps happen more often.
"Shoot for the Stars" makes a slick slogan—but a disappointing
delivery goal.

You see people bench themselves or leave early for the showers all too often when they set unrealistic goals. Take diets, for
example. The person who decides she'll lose fifty pounds in the
next two months dooms herself to failure. The regimen of an
hour's exercise in the morning, an hour's exercise in the evening,
and a 500-calorie-a-day diet lasts about two weeks or less.

At work, you can rarely increase revenue by 600 percent, build
an infrastructure, and retrain 70 percent of your team all in the
same quarter. So shoot for inches of improvement.

> *My mother drew a distinction between achievement and*
> *success. She said that achievement is the knowledge that*
> *you studied and worked hard and have done the best that*

is in you. Success is being praised by others, and that's nice,
too, but not as important or satisfying. Always aim for
achievement and forget about success.   —HELEN HAYES

Don't confuse activity with results and contribution. Don't get me wrong—focusing on getting the fundamentals down pat is essential. But dribbling, passing, blocking, or rebounding doesn't put points on the scoreboard.

Over the years we have had a few account executives who became confused between sales activity and sales results. They spent their time entering names into the database, researching the prospect's organization, leaving voice mails, writing e-mails, sending out literature, making appointments, recording notes in the database—and then became satisfied with that activity, never turning the activity into revenue.

It happens in almost any job. As a manager, you can get caught up in hiring, training, record keeping, policy setting— and forget to look for ways to increase net profit by generating revenue or cutting expenses. As a team leader, you may get tapped for assembling a group, identifying resources, setting deadlines, managing budgets, scheduling and supervising a project—and fail to question whether the project can accomplish the big-picture goal. Individually, you can technically "do your job" (the assigned activities and responsibilities) but fail to take the initiative in looking for ways to increase your value to the organization.

Activity does not equal contribution.

In weekly staff meetings, during performance reviews, or at strategic planning meetings, does your dialogue sound to others like the coach talking to the sportscaster? Will your colleagues and clients still expect a win?

A round your place of business, are you considered a high scorer?

Do not let what you cannot do interfere with what
you can do. —JOHN WOODEN

✱ **As a Signature Star, Your Autograph Says You . . .**
Deliver results.

PART FIVE

RUN, PLAY HURT, OR SIT OUT— BUT DON'T WHINE

*G*rumbling players get traded. Unless you're on the inside circle, of course, it's hard to know which came first—the unhappy player or the dissatisfied coach.

But news starts to dribble to the press: The player would like to be closer to his parents back in his old hometown. The coach has his eye on a top draft choice. The player doesn't get along with a teammate. The coach thinks the teammate is doing a fine job. The player thinks he may retire next year. The coach prefers working with young kids right out of college so he can mold them from the ground up. The player feels that the owner hasn't lived up to his early promises about building a first-rate ball club by recruiting the best available talent. The coach thinks the player's age has become a real limiting factor for the future. The player thinks the coach has an ego problem.

All of a sudden there's an announcement that the player has been traded. The whining stops, and both sides can go about their business. The only problem is that several million households heard the ugly details during the process. Far better had they sat down in a room, hashed out their needs, wishes, and concerns, and parted as friends.

Stars in the workplace can learn much from sports celebrities about what not to do if they intend to create a positive work environment, supportive relationships, and a strong reputation.

TWENTY-EIGHT

PROTECT YOUR TRADEMARK

What do Hillary Clinton, Osama Bin Laden, O. J. Simpson, Donald Trump, Stephen King, Arnold Schwarzenegger, Katie Couric, Britney Spears, Jerry Jones, Oprah Winfrey, and Richard Wagoner have in common? A reputation. The vast majority of people haven't ever met them personally, so whether most people love them or hate them depends on their reputation—largely controlled by the media.

The Charlotte Sting. The Houston Rockets. Lisa Leslie. The Atlanta Hawks. Dennis Rodman. The Indiana Pacers. The Sacramento Monarchs. The Dallas Mavericks. David Robinson. The Milwaukee Bucks. The Memphis Grizzlies. Allen Iverson. The Utah Jazz. The Minnesota Timberwolves. Sheryl Swoopes. The Boston Celtics. The Denver Nuggets. Tim Duncan. The Los Angeles Lakers. The Connecticut Sun. The San Antonio Silver Stars. The Detroit Pistons. The New York Knicks. Karl Malone. The Phoenix Suns. The Seattle Storm.

Besides the fact that these are pro basketball teams and players, what do they have in common? They all conjure up a reputation in the mind of sports enthusiasts—either positive or negative, either experienced or inexperienced, either winners or losers, either All-American or an embarrassment. As an example, according to *Lindy's 2003–2004 Pro Basketball,* "[The Portland Trail Blazers] are known as the most dysfunctional team in the NBA, perhaps in all of sports." Deserved or undeserved, that's the widespread reputation.

Individuals can generate this kind of reputation as well—sometimes from brief personal encounters. That was the case with Donna Davidson (not her real name) at a large oil-tool company in Houston. The Human Resources manager received a call from a vice president, saying that he intended to establish a customer-service support center in the coming year. The vice president wanted the HR manager to begin the selection process for the director of this customer-service center, which would be a midmanagement position.

"My first choice for that position," the vice president continued, "is Donna Davidson."

"Donna Davidson? Did I hear you correctly?"

"Yes."

"She has no management experience."

"But she has people experience."

"How do you know her?"

"I first saw her in a meeting about two years ago. Her boss couldn't attend and sent her as his representative. She's bright. Articulate—expresses herself well. Handles people well. Thinks on her feet. I've been watching her. Those are exactly the skills needed to handle customers."

Donna got the job, jumping several pay grades in the process. Like the pro teams, she had a reputation.

Your reputation is your own trademark in your workplace. What is it, and what's it worth to you?

Identify your suitable trademarks. Back in 1997, The Washington Bullets changed their name to the Washington Wizards. Even though such a name change cost big bucks—new logo, new uniforms, new signage, new promotional items, new advertising, new PR—the team believed the change worth the cost to shed the negative image of violence associated with the word *bullets* and start afresh. Even high school teams consider a name, logo, colors, and uniforms worth spending time and money on for the impression they create.

Can you imagine how you might think of the Dallas Mavericks if they had decided to call themselves the Dallas Mosquitoes? Or if the Boston Celtics had named themselves the Boston Beans? Or if the Golden State Warriors had called themselves the Golden State Wimps?

When I ask, "Do you have any people or departments in your organizations that have a negative reputation?" names and stories pop up quickly.

- "Marketing's a whiny bunch. A project gets killed and they moan for a month."
- "Collections. They're good. Very good. A little aggressive sometimes. But very good."
- "You don't want to go to IT with a problem. They're nasty on the phone. Very unhelpful. They make you feel stupid for calling. Totally unresponsive."
- "Our sales team is young, inexperienced, very little formal training in sales. But very dedicated. They want to do well."
- "Training. Totally out of the loop. They sit and wait for the

phone to ring rather than get out and learn the business and find out what we need to do our business better and help us do it."

How did these groups earn their reputations? Based on the actions and words of individuals. One conversation, plus one action, plus one conversation, plus one action, all tied end to end. Individuals earn their reputations the same way. These comments highlight some of the stories tracked in more detail:

- "His division does well. It accounts for about 15 percent of our total revenue of the parent company, and that's impressive. But he, personally, has an uncooperative attitude with the rest of his peers in the other divisions. He tunes out meetings. Doesn't offer input. Seems bored. He's not contributing the value we expect from people at the VP level."
- "She's the best project manager we have in the company— as far as getting a project done, within specs, on time, within budget. But we're about to terminate her because nobody wants to work with her. She alienates everybody she needs to cooperate with her on the inside. Only the outside suppliers who need our business tolerate her."
- "Auditing is a tough function anyway. But it's not just the position. He's defensive about everything. It's his attitude and his communication style. He talks down to people. He goes off on people without having all the facts. Goes over their heads to try to solve a problem rather than just trying to talk to the person involved. He does not take the time to establish rapport with people."

When your own team, department, or organization is named, what do others think of? How about your name individually? Is the image positive or a negative? Should you be concerned? Is this helping or hurting your efforts to deliver results and your ability to feel satisfaction in your job and life?

A good name is more desirable than great riches.

—PROVERBS 22:1

Register your trademarks. To get a registered trademark, you have to prove that you use the mark in your business by providing four samples of that use with your application. For example, to register trademarks on our proprietary training concepts, we included samples of their use on job-aid cards, pages from our training workbooks, pages from our published texts, keynote titles on our company stationery, and references in our video demos. We had to prove that we use the concepts routinely in order to protect them.

After you make up your mind how you want to be known—prove your reputation or "trademark" by living it consistently. Your reputation stems from what you say and what you do over time. Just as with a trademark, to "register" a reputation with your colleagues, you have to build it by use every day, hallway conversation after conversation, meeting after meeting, project after project. It's not a one-time shot.

Protect your trademarks. If you don't protect your registered trademark, you can lose it legally. That is, if someone steals your trademark and you know it but do nothing to protest that use, the courts may rule that you obviously no longer consider the trademark of value to you and that it has slipped into the public domain.

Likewise, when someone tries to steal your reputation, protect it. Of course, on minor issues, if the hurt and harm are minor, ignore what you can. Although frustration can be acute, the tit-for-tat urge is not a positive solution.

But if you think your personal integrity or credibility is at stake, take action. When you're the subject of harmful gossip or inappropriate action, set the record straight. Go to the person involved and explain that you have heard that they've said such and such and that you just want to set the record straight and assume they won't be saying or doing any more about the situation since they now know the accurate details (or complete story). Many people will deny the talk, but they will stop once they know you have identified them as the source.

If you think your reputation may be damaged with others (your boss, coworkers, family, friends), you may want to talk to them also. Don't assume the posture of "reporting" on the other person, but simply explain that you want them to know the full situation and circumstances so they can help you set the record straight if it comes up in other conversations. Then take comfort in God's promise that he will set the situation straight over the long haul.[1]

Use Your Trademarks. Trademarks open doors. They sell products. They assure quality. They give buyers confidence. A Hallmark logo on a greeting card sample tells retailers that the cards they order and stock in their stores will arrive in top quality condition. They don't have to worry that every fifth card in the boxes will have ink smudges and discolorations. When parents see the Good Housekeeping Seal of Approval on a new toy, they toss it in the shopping cart without much thought about its safety. Trademarks have power.

Likewise, you can use your protected good name as a powerful force in creating a positive culture. Use it to open doors, sell ideas, model an ethical stance, assure quality, and give confidence. Make your name mean something.

Ball clubs pay big money for names and logos to create an instant reputation—which can be lost in a season. Your reputation can be created for free—but it takes a lifetime.

When your name is mentioned around your organization, what three adjectives come to your coworkers' minds?

Reputation is what you need to get a job; character is what you need to keep it.   —UNKNOWN

✳ **As a Signature Star, Your Autograph Says You . . .**
Establish a positive reputation that opens doors.

TWENTY-NINE

TOSS THE BALL HIGHER
ON THE TIE-UPS

If you've ever played a pickup game of basketball, then you've probably seen a jump-ball scramble repeat itself two or three times before the inexperienced ref got a toss-up high enough and straight enough to clear both players. And the tougher the competition between the two opponents, the more the ref seems to struggle in keeping the ball in neutral territory.

Your role as a mediator with your coworkers doesn't get any easier. But part of creating a positive culture is helping to connect other members of the team when their own lines of communication close down. Here's what you can do to help minimize any grumbling and ill-thought-out trades among the players.

Avoid taking sides around the circle and talking the opposition over to the other viewpoint. Work with both individuals from the very beginning. You may decide to meet with both people together or separately. If you decide to meet with each separately, be sure both understand that what they share with you may not necessarily be withheld from the other person. You will have to use information from one person to verify and clarify with the other. If you don't warn them up front, they may lose confidence in your impartiality and think you are breaking their confidences.

Play sportscaster. You can only begin to make sense of someone else's conflict when armed with the unbiased versions of events and circumstances. An even better approach than asking the two people involved is to casually observe how "innocent bystanders" react to the situation and listen to what they have to say about the issues. Be careful, of course, that you don't just collect the data that was passed on to them from the other people directly involved. Probe for what they know or have observed firsthand. Identify facts, assumptions, assertions, and feelings. They all count.

Play press agent and handle the PR. If you can pass on complimentary remarks from the current discussions with each person, do so. If not, you may have to dig into the past to find these gems. "Jerry, Tonia does respect your work. If you recall, last quarter she asked to be assigned to your team on the Bilcox project." Or: "Lisa agrees that you've always been fair in dealings with her, that you've never tried to force her to travel on projects that she felt another staff member could handle. She appreciates your sensitivity on that issue."

The purpose of passing on such comments is to help them recall their past good relationship, if there has been one. Sharing positive remarks adds credence to other things the person says. If someone is honest and willing to admit or confirm the good, chances are they'll be honest—as they see it—about the problem.

Offer to coach. Restate their common goals—again and again. Examples: "Alison, Eric, both of you want to see this client go through the installation without any hiccups in the system. You both have some creative ideas to contribute about how we should analyze their datasets and balance their channel usage. Both of you want to protect the client's privacy and both of you want to retain the client's goodwill." Or: "Omar, you're concerned with cutting costs in this division this quarter. Bianca, you have the same mind-set—get the bottom line back in the black."

They need constant reminders of where they're going—the finish line. This step is particularly important if the mediation has taken several days or even weeks. Make sure both people know without a doubt what they each hope to accomplish from the situation or relationship. Act as their coach to get them down the court toward the goal.

Officiate. If either person balks during your role as coach, then as a last resort, you'll need to officiate on the tie-up:

1. Point out where you believe both people have miscommunicated in the past. You may decide to call both together at this point, if you've not already done so. After all your searching and probing into the problem, share your conclusions. Be straightforward. Point out their invalid assumptions about each other's actions, conversations with double meanings, and perceived intentions, along with your judgments and labels on those intentions. This will be the toughest part of your task as mediator. But Proverbs offers hope if your words are well chosen: "Good judgment proves that you are wise, and if you speak kindly, you can teach others."[1]

At the least, ask each person to paraphrase to you how he or she thinks the other views things and how he or she feels about those events or circumstances.

2. Advocate "no-fault" resolution. When a third party is involved, such as yourself, the people in conflict have an added

investment in maintaining their self-esteem. It's bad enough to admit error or fault to one person; it's doubly difficult to admit it to two people. Therefore, take every precaution to downplay any effort to affix blame.

Say it loudly, clearly, and frequently: "Conflict is inevitable. No one has to be at fault. Conflict just is. Let's focus on working out a resolution." And then make sure your phrasing supports that premise. Avoid questions like "Then what caused/made you think that?" "So if Cary hadn't done X, then Sarah wouldn't have done Y." Forget cause and effect for purposes of officiating in this game.

3. Ask those involved to suggest resolutions. If you suggest the resolution, it will be perceived as yours, not theirs. After clarifying the facts, identifying the misunderstandings, summarizing each person's needs, and reminding both of their goals, ask them for suggestions to resolve their differences. If necessary, reiterate their mutual criteria for coming to a resolution. As suggestions meet the criteria, accept them, record them, and ask for reaction from the other person. Accept. Check for agreement. Accept. Check for agreement.

4. Lead them to select the solution that best meets the needs of both. Your presence ensures that one person does not overpower the other. Your job as an impartial mediator who cares about both individuals is to see that the solution is acceptable to both, not a "win" for one and a "withdrawal" for the other.

Blessed are the peacemakers.   MATTHEW 5:9, KJV

When there's a tie-up and you care about the culture you're creating among your coworkers, help both to keep the lines of communication open. Pass on good news and compliments from one to the other. If you've been successful in helping them through a crisis, they'll rely on you again and again. And you'll have the satisfaction of knowing you've deactivated a productivity problem and kept one more relationship intact.

When coworkers are caught in conflict, do you know how to lead them to resolution without getting trapped in the conflict? Do you *care*—or do you just stay clear?

Never judge a person's actions until you know their motives.

—UNKNOWN

✳ **As a Signature Star, Your Autograph Says You . . .**
Know how to mediate conflict in a way that leaves relationships intact.

THIRTY

TURN HECKLERS INTO FANS

Opponents on the basketball court are to be expected. They have a different agenda, a different goal, and their own cheering section. It's not about you. It's just all about them.

But hecklers in the crowd raise hackles on your neck for an altogether different reason: It's not about them, it's all about you. They're tossing peanuts and popcorn at you. They're shooting spit wads at you. They're shouting insults at you. The game can get really ugly if the ref doesn't handle the situation.

The problem is there are no refs in the workplace. And even if there were, they might have a hard time given that everyone on the scene is wearing the same uniform. So to create and keep a positive culture where you can deliver results, it's up to you yourself to turn your hecklers into fans.

"Why bother?" some argue. "I do my job, stay out of other people's way. I don't care what other people think. Isn't my performance ultimately what counts?"

Results contribute to reputation, sure. But results do not necessarily equate to all that your organization expects of you.

As a person of influence, you have more to contribute than simply work-related competencies. Additionally, a Signature Star has a mission in the workplace—a calling to do the highest quality work and to attract others to faith in God. And that mission is difficult to accomplish when people don't like you.

START THE CLOCK

When you don't know all the facts causing a specific conflict with another individual or group, you may need to dwell on the problem: When did the problem occur? Why is A or B a problem at all? How is the problem affecting others? How much is the problem costing in time, effort, and money? But once all the information comes to the forefront, move to a solution-centered discussion. Devise alternatives. Identify methods. Make comparisons and contrasts. Evaluate the effort or costs. Propose solutions. Avoid analysis paralysis. In short, move from "study" to "act."

Go back to the X's and O's. Redraw your game plays to create new alternatives. Define together what success will look like to everybody involved in the ongoing conflict. Then work backward. Can we change the deadline? Can we expand or cut the budget? Can we change the specifications? Can we alter the process? Can we break things into more doable chunks? Can we get more people involved? Should we have fewer people involved? Can we reverse the steps required? Can we redefine the problem altogether? Should we use different criteria to judge the resolution?

Don't let them fool you. Inattention is the least expensive, easiest, and fastest weapon used to control a power play—an unreasonable demand or threat. If you don't believe it, watch a server at your local restaurant or a flight attendant on your next airplane trip handle an obnoxious customer that way. Simply

ignore a person's unreasonable requests, threats, or demands
until they change their mind and pass the ball to another player.
The writer of Proverbs chalks up silence to character: "It's a mark
of good character to avert quarrels, but fools love to pick fights."[1]

Identify who's playing defense. Tone and inflection in the English language can be subtle, yet they pack a walloping punch. Take
these examples: "What proof do you have?" can be a straightforward request for more explanation or a challenge, meaning that
you're making unfounded allegations. "I don't know what you're
talking about" can mean "That's nonsense" or "I'm puzzled."
"Earlier you said X; now you're saying Y" can mean "I think you're
lying" or can mean "I'm confused; please sort out the seeming con-
tradiction so I can follow." Such lines can escalate conversations
into arguments. Tone, mood, and attitude all convey meaning.

The difficulty is deciding who is being defensive. Who is
"reading into" the conversation. If you're the one on the defensive, you're likely to hear double meanings in straightforward
requests and statements. If the other person is on the defensive,
he or she will let the defensive tone creep in and then deny it
when challenged.

Instead of sorting out a problem by starting with the words,
start with the attitude. Decide who has the defensive attitude,
and then determine the meaning of the words. It's a remarkably
reliable system for resolving conflicts that originate because of
personality issues.

Discard the old cheerleading chant about sticks and stones.
Since childhood, we've heard the axiom, "Sticks and stones may
break my bones, but names will never hurt me." Our parents
taught us the chant as a defense mechanism for use when some
neighborhood bully overpowered us with words. It might have

worked as children but not as adults. Words do damage relationships forever. The most painful memories many of us have
involve what someone said to us. "I lost control" is no excuse.
According to Proverbs, "Hot tempers start fights; a calm, cool
spirit keeps the peace."[2] The tongue as a weapon can destroy a
reputation, a career, or a person.

Take care not to charge the other shooter. Prefer statements
to questions during conflict. By the time you decide to discuss
a conflict openly, trust has usually fallen and tensions have risen.
Questions will be suspect from either side. Why? Because most
will contain accusations. "Why did you not tell me you wanted
these by Friday?" "How did you think we could spend that kind
of money on this project?" Granted, these may be informational
questions—but they won't sound like it when there's tension and
resentment in the air.

Instead, make statements about what you feel or think.
"I would have appreciated advance notice that these items were
needed by Friday." Or, "I think we can get this project done on
a much smaller budget than the $10,000 you recommended
in your report." Ask questions only when you really are trying
to gather information: "Is the deadline Thursday or Friday?"
"Do you know if we have a budget to use outside help?"

A statement usually generates a response—either agreement
or disagreement. An accusing question usually generates a
confrontation.

Trade goals at halftime. Just to make sure neither team has an
advantage with lighting, drafts, sound, view of the scoreboard or
clock, teams trade goals midway through the game so they're
forced to play the game and see the court from two viewpoints.
That's not a bad idea in any conflict.

Don't assume that the other person understands your point of view. No matter if you think the issues and repercussions of someone's actions are obvious, state them. Don't assume. What is obvious to you is not necessarily obvious to the other person.

Decide where your uniforms match. Define the areas of agreement or disagreement. Good negotiators work from a successful starting point: They start on the easy issues and move to the more difficult points. Likewise, when discussing a conflict, begin by confirming the areas of agreement. That might mean confirming undisputed facts or shared goals for the outcome. Finding that you do agree on some issues gives momentum to take you through the harder issues.

Kill the chatter that chills. Eliminate argumentative words and phrases. Examples: "That's not true." "You're wrong." "You're confused." "You don't know what you're talking about." "That's a half-baked idea if I ever heard one!" Proverbs says that a soft answer will turn away anger.[3] Any of the above sentiments can be expressed in a more acceptable, less abrasive way: "My facts don't agree with those." "I disagree." "There's some confusion here." "There are some issues you may not be aware of." "I don't think that idea will work." Avoid "fighting" words unless you want to fight.

Realize that some games end in a tie. Both sides—with differing viewpoints—can be right. Consider the sharp disagreement that rose between Paul and Barnabas after their first missionary journey, when they took young John Mark along with them. Paul's position with this issue sounded something like this: "Look, Barney, John Mark's got of lot of growing up to do. He still gets homesick—he deserted us in Pamphylia and went home. We don't have time for this sort of thing. The Lord's coming back, and we need to tell the world. Leave the kid at home another few years." Barnabas's position on the issue may have sounded something like this: "Paul, have a little heart. We're supposed to be mentoring this preacher-in-the-making. Even if he is young, he can be a lot of help to us."[4]

Both made a valid point. And God worked good out of the conflict. Two missionary teams rose out of that disagreement: Barnabas took John Mark and Paul teamed up with Silas for the next trip.

People bring different backgrounds, values, roles, experiences, and goals to the workplace. Not all differences can be reconciled. Policy A may be bad for Joe and good for Manuel. Alan may want to be rewarded with plenty of time off the job while Katherine may insist on stock options. Neither opinions—nor goals—are necessarily wrong.

Both may be very right and appropriate—and the cause of conflict. It's a fact of life difficult to accept but necessary to your sanity.

I am at peace with God. My conflict is with man.
—CHARLIE CHAPLIN

PICK UP THE EXTRA POINT WHEN SHOOTING BEHIND THE ARC

Working under the pressure of personal conflict adds distance to your reach for the goal—much like shooting from behind the arc. An operational manager almost missed a valuable idea because of such emotional clutter: the tiresomeness of dealing with an abrasive worker with an abrupt communication style. The worker made a valid suggestion on a project. But the manager jumped to

a conclusion and decided to tune him out rather than hear him—
simply because it was an emotional shortcut through the din of
other duties calling for his attention.

The apostle Paul admonishes us, "If it is possible, as far as it
depends on you, live at peace with everyone."[5] Though this might
seem like an improbable goal, God didn't put us on our own.
Proverbs says, "When a man's ways are pleasing to the Lord, he
makes even his enemies live at peace with him."[6]

Notice that the Bible didn't say that everyone will like us. Jesus
said, "If you find the godless world is hating you, remember it got
its start hating me."[7] Some people will disagree with and dislike
every value and belief you hold sacred. But God did command us
to *try* to keep peace with everyone. And there is a difference.

Personal conflict can cost you peace of mind, break your concentration on important goals, and blind you to bonanzas or bumps
along the way. Instead of making it all about you, try to make
your response all about them. The other person's needs. The
other person's goals. The other person's self-respect.

*W*hat conflict is keeping you from doing your best work? How can you resolve it?

---

*Learn the wisdom of compromise, for it is better to bend
a little than to break.*   —JANE WELLS

✳ As a Signature Star, Your Autograph Says You . . .
Resolve personal conflict that breaks your concentration.

THIRTY-ONE

DON'T WAIT FOR THE REF TO THROW YOU OUT OF THE GAME

It happens in all sports; basketball is no exception. A player gets upset and begins to mouth off to the ref. The ref blows a whistle and calls a technical foul. Then the upset player becomes even more indignant. The coach and teammates take sides, either encouraging the flare-up or trying to calm it. The ref calls another technical foul on the coach.

The player and coach have a choice at that moment: Either earn another technical and get thrown out of the game or shut their mouths.

But bad things can happen in a ball game or a season through no fault of your own. A defender can trip you and cause you to twist a knee and be out for the season. A teammate can jump into you on a rebound, come down on top of your foot, and crack it in three places. Criminal actions of a teammate can cast a negative shadow on the entire team. A messy media matter involving a coach can sour the press's attitude toward the entire team. Injuries and sickness can keep your team out of the play-offs for the championship. A bad call by the referee can keep you from breaking a career scoring record.

Some situations are unfair; all are unfortunate. How you respond to each will determine if you stay on the court, who stays on the court with you, if you stay in the lineup for the season, if your team has a winning or losing season, and ultimately if you are forced to leave the league. Basically, you have three choices as a player: adapt where you are, ask to be traded, or exit the game for good. The grace with which you make your choice determines how you will be remembered.

It helps to consider these same principles in dealing with difficulties and disappointments at work:

1. You can adapt and work within the circumstances.
2. You can ask to be traded—find another role within your organization.
3. Or, you can exit the game—go somewhere else and find another league or sport.

CAN YOU ADAPT?

Remember that some games get postponed. In high-school play, occasionally, national emergencies or inclement weather lead to the cancellations of games that never get rescheduled. You have no chance to add another win to the record. You have no chance to improve your statistics for the season. The record stands as it is. Although pro leagues reschedule such cancelled games, their postponement typically sets up a different circumstance—with a different injury list and so forth.

Some issues and difficulties on the job are not within your power to resolve. For example, a merger that goes sour or an economic downturn in your industry. Some problems may be so difficult that their solutions, like a ballgame, will be "postponed and rescheduled" many times before they're instituted. Some may never be resolved. For example, poor decision making at the top may lead to a sudden fall in the value of your stock options or retirement account.

Other issues surface in some corner of the court in almost every organization: Again, the Bible, the ultimate playbook, provides insight about responding in these situations:

Bosses who treat employees unfairly	"Do not withhold good from those who deserve it, when it is in your power to act."[1]
	"The world of the generous gets larger and larger; the world of the stingy gets smaller and smaller. The one who blesses others is abundantly blessed; those who help others are helped."[2]
Managers who put profits ahead of people	"People curse those who hold their grain for higher prices, but they bless the one who sells to them in their time of need."[3]
Angry, harsh bosses	"If your boss is angry with you, don't quit! A quiet spirit can overcome even great mistakes."[4]
	"Don't just do what you have to do to get by, but work heartily, as Christ's servants doing what God wants you to do. And work with a smile on your face, always keeping in mind that no matter who happens to be giving the orders, you're really serving God."[5]
	"Faithful messengers are as refreshing as snow in the heat of summer. They revive the spirit of their employer."[6]
Disloyal, disrespectful employees	"If you honor your boss, you'll be honored."[7]
Lazy employees	"The desires of lazy people will be their ruin, for their hands refuse to work."[8]
	"A lazy person has trouble all through life; the path of the upright is easy!"[9]

	"If you are too lazy to plow, don't expect a harvest."[10]
	"Anyone too lazy to cook will starve, but a hard worker is a valuable treasure."[11]
	"Lazy people are soon poor; hard workers get rich. Lazy people are a pain to their employer. They are like smoke in the eyes or vinegar that sets the teeth on edge."[12]
	"The diligent find freedom in their work; the lazy are oppressed by work."[13]
Employees who do not do quality work	"Bad work gets paid with a bad check; good work gets solid pay."[14]
	"The one who stays on the job has food on the table; the witless chase whims and fancies."[15]
Coworkers with explosive tempers	"Watch your words and hold your tongue; you'll save yourself a lot of grief."[16]
Haughty, proud colleagues	"Don't bother talking sense to fools; they'll only poke fun at your words."[17]
	"Do not gloat when your enemy falls; when he stumbles, do not let your heart rejoice."[18]
	"The stuck-up fall flat on their faces, but down-to-earth people stand firm."[19]
Negative, complaining colleagues	"Everyone enjoys a fitting reply; it is wonderful to say the right thing at the right time!"[20]
	"Worry is a heavy burden, but a kind word always brings cheer."[21]
	"Some people make cutting remarks, but the words of the wise bring healing."[22]
	"Do not extort money from anyone by threats or by false accusation, and be content with your wages."[23]
Gossips	"A gossip betrays a confidence; so avoid a man who talks too much."[24]
	"Dishonest people use gossip to destroy their neighbors; good people are protected by their own good sense. . . . It's stupid to say bad things about your neighbors. If you are sensible, you will keep quiet."[25]
People who lie	"The Lord hates those who don't keep their word, but he delights in those who do."[26]

Those with dishonest business practices	"Do not cheat or rob anyone. Always pay your hired workers promptly."[27]
	"God cares about honesty in the workplace; your business is his business. Good leaders abhor wrongdoing of all kinds; sound leadership has a moral foundation."[28]
	"The integrity of the upright guides them, but the unfaithful are destroyed by their duplicity."[29]
	"Whoever can be trusted with very little can also be trusted with much, and whoever is dishonest with very little will also be dishonest with much."[30]

If you work in a culture where any of the above are consistent problems, then like injured ballplayers, you have to decide whether you want to stay in the game and play hurt. You either ask to be taken out of the game or you stay and tough it out. If you stay, you'll know that you've made a conscious choice not to complain to your coworkers but to work to influence others and create a positive culture within the circumstances to make the goal.

Mouthing off at the ref typically results in bringing teammates into the fray and threatens to jeopardize the game for everybody. And besides that, it's embarrassing to get charged with a technical and get sent to the showers. Whining wins few friends and rarely earns respect.

DO YOU WANT TO BE TRADED?

Nothing will discourage you more than spending eight to twelve hours of your allotted twenty-four-hour day doing something that you dislike in a difficult situation in exchange for a mere paycheck. I'm not necessarily talking about a complete career change—changing your life's work from practicing law to teaching art. But perhaps a minor shift is all it would take to move you off the hectic track of hassles into a more satisfying position.

For example, instead of selling insurance, you may want to conduct seminars for your new agents, teaching them the insurance industry. Instead of managing the corporate public affairs department, you may want to consult with top officials of your organization who regularly meet the press. Instead of school administration as high-school principal, you may want to move into the classroom.

A senior manager at a large telecommunications company recently told me about his goal to build morale when he took over a new group. People felt discouraged, burned out, overworked, and angry. He made it his mission to assess their strengths, ask them what they really wanted to do, shuffle their responsibilities, and move them into jobs they really enjoyed. Several corporations today try to offer employees many different jobs through the course of their career—even if it means moving laterally or relocating across the world.

Such changes may mean shorter hours, more or less travel, more or less people contact, more personal growth opportunities, more or less routine, more or less creative challenge, less responsibility and stress, greater personal satisfaction.

Rather than make a scene and go to the showers in a huff, just quietly start talks about a trade and see where you might like to play your next game.

DO YOU WANT TO FIND ANOTHER LEAGUE OR SPORT?

If you can't adjust to the circumstances, coach, coworkers, and rules in your league and sport, maybe you should consider an exit. If you can't be passionate about your work, find a way to make your passion your work.

That's what Mike and Tracey Nosko did. The military stationed Mike in Alaska, and he loved life in the outdoors there. When they wanted to move him back to the Lower 48, he balked. What he really enjoys is breeding and training huskies. His dream became to win the Iditarod more times than anyone else. When there for one of his dogsled rides, I visited with his wife, Tracey. "So what do you and Mike do to make a living while you're waiting for the once-a-year competition?"

She laughed. "I work for the post office. He has a career a week. Shoveling snow on contract. Driving a school bus. Construction. Whatever gives him a paycheck for the week and doesn't cut into his time training the dogs. He's driven by that passion."

Rather than staying trapped and miserable in a difficult situation and alienating all those around you, choose to leave. Find another league or a new sport in which to excel.

When bad things happen and you decide to play hurt, adapt so that you can influence others positively. If you ask to be traded or exit, do so with class. Your team and the fans will remember well the ruckus or ratings of your last game.

*W*hat is your most difficult conflict? Are you going to play hurt, ask to be traded, or exit? If you choose to stay in the game and play hurt, how are you going to heal the situation?

Pick battles big enough to matter, small enough to win.

—JONATHAN KOZOL

✷ **As a Signature Star, Your Autograph Says You . . .**
Take your tumbles, adapt, or exit with class.

PART SIX

SIGN ON FOR LIFE

*W*hen you think of your sport as a career, you approach things differently. You're not capitalizing solely on your strengths; you need to turn your weaknesses into pluses as well. You're not looking for a coach who'll make you feel important; you want a coach who will challenge you. You're not focusing on winning one big championship title; you want to sign with a team that provides a lifetime of championship opportunities. You're not focusing on the season's stats; you're focusing on life-time achievement records.

The same holds true in pursuing God's best at work. You're not focusing on a job; you're focusing on building character in the job. You're not focusing solely on income; you're focusing also on impact. You're not focusing only on a career; you're focusing on making a contribution in your calling.

THIRTY-TWO

ENJOY YOUR OFF-SEASON

The injured high-school player came off the court with blood
streaming from a cut across the corner of his eye. The coach took
one look at him and shouted, "That's two feet from your heart.
Get back in there and play!"

The player grabbed a towel, mopped the stream of red from
his forehead, and trotted back onto the court. Taking his place
along the free-throw lane, he flinched at the pain, and then
lunged for the rebound. They needed him, and he didn't intend
to let his buddies down.

The high-school team struggled to field a team year after year,
where five farming communities came together to form one
consolidated district. When flu season hit, they stood a strong
chance of forfeiting important district games and possibly the
entire season because they didn't have enough players to suit up.

While the coach's comment may have been motivating to the
eighteen-year-old, it may not have been the smartest thing to do
for his long-term health. However, 38-, 48-, and 58-year-olds are
still making the same decisions. They work at their job until

they're physically spent. But because they feel needed, they're motivated to overwork until they burn out and lose everything— their job, their health, their relationships, and their fellowship with God.

Ballplayers, coaches, and team owners understand the importance of an off-season to prevent burnout.

But the off-season serves other purposes as well: High schoolers use the off-season to play different sports so they can explore other talents and interests. Often, at this age, athletes play and letter in two, three, or even four sports. College athletes, too, enjoy the off-season to "catch up" in their lives— to socialize and date, to take extra, difficult courses and "get them out of the way," to reconsider their academic majors, and to investigate their options for the pros.

Unlike these younger players, pro athletes have settled on their sport. But that doesn't mean they don't make good use of their off-season. In fact, what they do during the off-season may be the most important part of their overall career longevity and lifetime earning power. Typically, it's during the off-season that they negotiate new business deals such as product endorsements, set up other financial investments and partnerships for the future, and take care of their agent relationships. And, of course, they interact with their social networks, rest, and give injuries time to heal as well.

All workers—whatever their game—need an off-season. As a country, we're just now discovering how badly we need that off-season. Mary Barnett Gilson, economist and educator, observed more than sixty-five years ago: "Work is only part of a man's life; play, family, church, individual and group contacts, educational opportunities, the intelligent exercise of citizenship, all play a part in a well-rounded life. Workers are men and women with potentialities for mental and spiritual development as well as for physical health. We are paying the price today of having too long sidestepped all that this means to the mental, moral, and spiritual health of our nation."[1] What would she say today, sixty-five years further down the road?

What you do with your own personal downtime will determine your satisfaction and success during the regular season and over a lifetime.

Stay in shape physically. A pastor friend of mine fondly warns members of his congregation, "God told us to rest one day a week. You can do it like he said, or you can wind up taking your days all in a row—in the hospital." Even Jesus, as important as his mission was and with an urgent deadline looming, took time for rest. He withdrew from the crowds on occasion and found time alone to pray and rest. It's worth a note in passing, however, that rest doesn't necessarily mean to stop all activity. For you, it may simply mean the relaxation that comes from a change of pace.

But rest is not all that's involved in taking care of ourselves physically. In season, an athlete stays in shape by training, discipline, and diet, as well as proper sleep. In the off-season, they add a different component to the mix: more attention to injuries and corrective surgeries, and less discipline regarding training, diet, and sleep.

But the need to stay physically fit doesn't disappear. Players don't expect to gain fifty pounds during the few months of off-season business and entertaining and then be back in shape in a couple of weeks when the season starts. They maintain the discipline of general physical fitness year-round.

To enjoy your work for the long term, you have to do the

same. Your schedule and hours have to be reasonable enough to allow you to stay physically fit.

Get financially fit. Rather than working head down day after day after day, you need an off-season to set your financial house in order and keep the lawn well maintained. Even the wealthiest individuals don't just turn things over to a brokerage house or money manager and walk away. They keep an eye on what's happening in the world and how that might affect their investments.

Smart athletes manage their money well and invest wisely during their years of high-earning potential so that they can maintain their standard of living when they retire from the game. Financial fitness is less about income than "outgo." To be physically fit, focus on what you keep as well as what you earn.

Proverbs says, "A pretentious, showy life is an empty life; a plain and simple life is a full life."[2] In his best seller *The Purpose-Driven Life,* Rick Warren observes, "Purpose-driven living leads to a simpler lifestyle and a saner schedule. . . . You become effective by being selective." That saner lifestyle affects your finances by shrinking your outgo. Then with the outgo under control, you can set about investing the income well.

No matter how large or small your income, you need time to educate yourself about financial matters: your personal net worth, insurance issues, estate planning and wills, investing, giving. You'll need to read, listen to financial TV networks, and stay up to date on new laws and how they affect you.

Some people spend such long hours making their money that they have no time or energy left over to figure out how to manage it.

At the least, you'll need a quarterly off-season and an annual off-season to stay financially fit.

Grow your intellectual capital. Marriages often split when one partner wakes up one morning and decides he or she has "outgrown" the other. Yes, love commits to stay regardless. But how much happier the scene when both persons use their off-season to pursue projects that stimulate them intellectually and make them a more interesting person: reading, attending a class, learning a new skill, pursuing a hobby, meeting with a Bible-study group. Proverbs says, "An intelligent person is always eager to take in more truth; fools feed on fast-food fads and fancies."[3]

An extra benefit, of course, is that this off-season growth deepens your expertise and broadens your opportunity for career advancement.

Keep your social relationships intact. In his international best seller *Emotional Intelligence,* Daniel Goleman discusses the limited future of individuals, no matter how high their IQ, who lack innate interpersonal skills (what he dubbed their EQ, emotional quotient). My work as a consultant to Fortune 500 companies during the past twenty-four years substantiates the same limitations. University recruiters have understood the principle for years, preferring to give scholarships to B students with broad interests and many activities during high school, rather than to A students focused solely on their academic work.

Even Jesus took time out of his brief three-year mission on earth to socialize. The Bible records several instances where he attended weddings, funerals, and meals at the homes of friends.

When work becomes so all-consuming that your social calendar centers totally around work relationships and obligations, your quality of life will suffer. Inevitably, work friends talk about work. And if there's stress from an issue at work, that stress will spill over into your social conversations so that you can't get

away from the problem even after hours. You need the stimula-
tion of friends involved in other pursuits and interests. They
share a different perspective and pace.

Todd Szalkowski talks of how he has rounded out his life to
enjoy his off-season: "I used to work twelve hours a day routinely.
Now I come in to work at seven fifteen and leave at five fifteen.
I coach my kids in their sports teams. My marriage is stronger.
I'm more active at church, on committees. I teach Bible study
on Sunday morning. I've always had a desire to make Christ the
center of my life, but I'd just never taken the steps to carry it out.
Of course, I'm still available to clients by cell. But once I put my
time and money in order, everything else fell in place."

Take note when your friends stop calling. Ask yourself how
long it has been since you hosted guests for dinner. When these
other relationships fall by the wayside, your life is careening out
of balance. You need a longer off-season.

To enjoy the game of work, guard your off-season. While it's
nice to feel perpetually needed on the court, it's nicer to feel
physically rested, financially fit, and personally well-rounded
in your pursuits.

Who are you when you're not working?

---

*To be able to fill leisure intelligently is the last product of
civilization, and at present very few people have reached
this level.*
                                                            —BERTRAND RUSSELL

✳ **As a Signature Star, Your Autograph Says You . . .**
Keep yourself physically fit, financially fit, intellectually challenged, and socially well-rounded.

THIRTY-THREE

MULTIPLY YOUR ENDORSEMENT OFFERS

The mega basketball stars turn their celebrity status into a wider platform with endorsement offers and honorary titles. You hear them singing TV jingles for salsa and chips. You see their smiling faces on billboards advertising long-distance phone service. You see them striding across magazine ads for running shoes. You try on their line of jogging suits or buy their autographed books in the mall. You give to the charities that borrow their name for their posters.

Competence gains attention. Competence plus character creates influence.

It's true in sports and in most every field. Our job is to make sure it's true of us.

What if all those who come in contact with us at work had the same reaction as those who worked with Daniel, administrator in King Darius's court in what is now Iraq? Here's the way the Bible describes Daniel's work and his reputation with colleagues:

"Daniel soon proved himself more capable than all the other

administrators and princes. Because of his great ability, the king made plans to place him over the entire empire. Then the other administrators and princes began searching for some fault in the way Daniel was handling his affairs, but they couldn't find anything to criticize. He was faithful and honest and always responsible. So they concluded, 'Our only chance of finding grounds for accusing Daniel will be in connection with the requirements of his religion.'"[1]

Would your colleagues and clients say the same about you? Imagine having our supervisors and coworkers say they could find no fault whatsoever in our work, character, or habits in any regard? That would certainly gain us a platform to share our faith and values. Instead, here are typical comments about coworkers: "He's a great guy, a good friend. But I wouldn't want to have him leading our company." Or, "She's an ace engineer—but just not the kind of person you'd want to have for a friend." Or, "He has skills we need on the team, but you don't want to be around him long or he'll start to get on your nerves with his constant complaining."

Have you ever wondered about the size of your personal platform at work? If you have earned personal influence because of the way you work, have you ever made a commitment to use your influence to lead others to faith in God?

> *Every action of our lives touches some chord that will vibrate in eternity.*   —UNKNOWN

Todd Szalkowski remembers a wake-up call several years ago from a group of friends who meet together to encourage and hold each other accountable for living out their faith in their daily lives. "My friends began to ask me, 'What do you speak more passionately about—golf or God?'

"I had to stop and honestly ask myself that question: When other people talk to me, what do they talk to me about? That'll give us a clue about what comes to mind when others think of us—and where our priorities are."

It's a good question for all of us: What do you speak most passionately about when you're with your friends at work? If your coworkers have a problem and sense that God might be the answer, would they come to you to discuss the issue? Would your speech, attitudes, habits, and competence you've shown on the job discourage them from coming to you at all?

As a Signature Star, ask God to multiply your endorsement offers with greater opportunities to influence because of your work interactions.

*I*s your platform of influence expanding?

_____

> *Example is not the main thing in influencing others.*
> *It is the only thing.*   —UNKNOWN

_____

✷ As a Signature Star, Your Autograph Says You . . .
Influence others by your competence and character at work.

NOTES

Chapter 1: Sign Up for the Season
1. Ecclesiastes 9:10, NLT.

Chapter 2: Focus on Offense, Not Defense
1. International Organization for Standardization.
2. See Matthew 22:36-40.

Chapter 3: Suit Up
1. Jack Welch, *Jack: Straight from the Gut* (New York: Warner Books, 2001), 24.
2. Danny Cox with John Hoover, *Leadership When the Heat's On* (New York: McGraw, 2002), 6.

Chapter 4: Learn More Than One Play
1. Bavendam Research Study, conducted among fifteen thousand largely white-collar workers from all levels of the participating organizations. Twenty percent were managers/supervisors; 91% were full-time workers; average age was thirty-three, with an even proportion of males and females.
2. Philippians 4:11.
3. See Acts 17:16-33.
4. John 8:7
5. Mark 9:40.

Chapter 7: Play Your Position
1. Romans 14:12, NLT.
2. The Parable of the Talents; Matthew 25:14-30; Luke 19:12-27.

Chapter 9: Take Your Shot
1. Oren Harari, *The Powell Principles* (New York: McGraw, 2002), e-book.

Chapter 10: Admit Your Fouls
1. 1 Chronicles 21:8.
2. Proverbs 28:13, NLT.

Chapter 12: Play by the Rules
1. *Fort Worth Star Telegram*, September 15, 2003.

2. PricewaterhouseCoopers, *Global Economic Crime Survey 2003,*
www.pwcglobal.com/extweb/ncsurvres.nsf/docid/
65EC95F223DCDAD785256D4D004ECD3E.

Chapter 13: Find Cheerleaders
1. Hebrews 12:1, *The Message.*

Chapter 14: Develop a Playbook
1. Isaiah 14:26-27.
2. Genesis 41:28-36.
3. Nehemiah 2:11-17.
4. Esther 4–5.
5. Acts 15:36; 20:1-16; 21:1-15.
6. Luke 14:28-30.
7. 1 Chronicles 28:19.
8. Proverbs 14:8, NLT.
9. Proverbs 22:3, NLT.
10. Proverbs 27:23.
11. Proverbs 3:5-6, NLT.

Chapter 16: Scrimmage
1. 1 Corinthians 9:24-25.

Chapter 18: Call a Huddle
1. American Management Association, www.amanet.org, "AMA 2002 Survey
on Internal Collaboration."
2. Jack Welch, *Jack: Straight from the Gut* (New York: Warner Books, 2001), 57.

Chapter 19: Keep Your Eye on the Ball
1. Roland Lazenby, "Yesterday and Today: A Conversation with Jerry West,"
Lindy's 2003–2004 Pro Basketball, 18.

Chapter 22: Slow the Tempo
1. Proverbs 18:15, CEV.
2. Proverbs 18:13.
3. Proverbs 18:17.
4. Proverbs 11:14, NLT.
5. James 1:5, NLT.
6. Proverbs 3:6, NLT.

Chapter 23: Make the Fast Break

1. See Genesis 39.
2. Deanna LaJune Laney, "Sheriff: Texas Woman Says God Told Her to Kill Sons," CNN.com, May 13, 2003.
3. See Matthew 4:18-22.
4. See Matthew 9:9.

Chapter 25: Take a Look-See

1. Proverbs 24:27.
2. Ecclesiastes 3:1-7.
3. See Nehemiah 2.
4. See Nehemiah 2:12-17.
5. Esther 4:14.

Chapter 28: Protect Your Trademark

1. See Romans 12:19.

Chapter 29: Toss the Ball Higher on the Tie-Ups

1. Proverbs 16:21, CEV.

Chapter 30: Turn Hecklers into Fans

1. Proverbs 20:3, *The Message*.
2. Proverbs 15:18, *The Message*. (Proverbs 12:16 is a similar saying.)
3. See Proverbs 15:1.
4. See Acts 15:37-40.
5. Romans 12:18.
6. Proverbs 16:7.
7. John 15:18, *The Message*.

Chapter 31: Don't Wait for the Ref to Throw You out of the Game

1. Proverbs 3:27.
2. Proverbs 11:24-25, *The Message*.
3. Proverbs 11:26, NLT.
4. Ecclesiastes 10:4, NLT.
5. Ephesians 6:6-7, *The Message*.
6. Proverbs 25:13, NLT.
7. Proverbs 27:18, *The Message*.
8. Proverbs 21:25, NLT.

9. Proverbs 15:19, NLT.

10. Proverbs 20:4, CEV.

11. Proverbs 12:27, CEV.

12. Proverbs 10:4, 26, NLT.

13. Proverbs 12:24, *The Message.*

14. Proverbs 11:18, *The Message.*

15. Proverbs 12:11, *The Message.*

16. Proverbs 21:23, *The Message.*

17. Proverbs 23:9, *The Message.*

18. Proverbs 24:17.

19. Proverbs 11:2, *The Message.*

20. Proverbs 15:23, NLT.

21. Proverbs 12:25, CEV.

22. Proverbs 12:18, NLT.

23. Luke 3:14, ESV.

24. Proverbs 20:19.

25. Proverbs 11:9-12, CEV.

26. Proverbs 12:22, NLT.

27. Leviticus 19:13, NLT.

28. Proverbs 16:11-12, *The Message.*

29. Proverbs 11:3.

30. Luke 16:10.

Chapter 32: Enjoy Your Off-Season

1. Mary Barnett Gilson, *What's Past Is Prologue* (New York: Arno Press, 1980, c1940), chap. 12.

2. Proverbs 13:7, *The Message.*

3. Proverbs 15:14, *The Message.*

Chapter 33: Multiply Your Endorsement Offers

1. Daniel 6:3-5, NLT.

RESOURCES BY DIANNA BOOHER AVAILABLE FROM BOOHER CONSULTANTS

BOOKS: Selected Titles

Your Signature Life: Pursuing God's Best Every Day

From Contact to Contract: 496 Proven Sales Tips to Generate More Leads, Close More Deals, Exceed Your Goals, and Make More Money

Speak with Confidence: Powerful Presentations That Inform, Inspire and Persuade

E-Writing: 21st Century Tools for Effective Communication

Communicate with Confidence®: How to Say It Right the First Time and Every Time

Fresh-Cut Flowers for a Friend

The Little Book of Big Questions: Answers to Life's Perplexing Questions

Good Grief, Good Grammar

To the Letter: A Handbook of Model Letters for the Busy Executive

Great Personal Letters for Busy People

The Complete Letterwriter's Almanac

Clean Up Your Act: Effective Ways to Organize Paperwork and Get It out of Your Life

Executive's Portfolio of Model Speeches for All Occasions

The New Secretary: How to Handle People as Well as You Handle Paper

Writing for Technical Professionals

Winning Sales Letters

Get a Life without Sacrificing Your Career

Ten Smart Moves for Women

Get Ahead, Stay Ahead

The Worth of a Woman's Words

Well Connected: Power Your Own Soul by Plugging into Others

Mother's Gifts to Me

The Esther Effect

Love Notes: From My Heart to Yours

First Thing Monday Morning

VIDEOS

Writing for Results

Writing in Sensitive Situations

Building Rapport with Your Customers

Giving and Receiving Feedback without Punching Someone Out!

Thinking on Your Feet: What to Say During Q&A

Basic Steps for Better Business Writing (series)

Business Writing: Quick, Clear, Concise

Closing the Gap: Gender Communication Skills

Cutting Paperwork: Management Strategies

Cutting Paperwork: Support Staff Strategies

AUDIOS

Get Your Book Published

People Power

Write to the Point: Business Communications from Memos to Meetings

E-LEARNING PROGRAMS

Selling Skills and Strategies: Write Proposals That Win the Business

*Selling Skills and Strategies: Thinking on Your Feet: Handling
    11 Difficult Question Types*

Selling Skills and Strategies: Write to Your Buyers: Email, Letters, Reports

Selling Skills and Strategies: Create and Deliver Sales Presentations with Impact

Selling Skills and Strategies: Negotiate So That Everyone Wins

Selling Skills and Strategies: Everyone Sells: Selling Skills for the Non-Salesperson

Selling Skills and Strategies: Manage Your Pipeline, Accounts, and Time

Effective Writing

Effective Editing

Good Grief, Good Grammar

More Good Grief, Good Grammar

Ready, Set, NeGOtiate

WORKSHOPS

Effective Writing

Technical Writing

Developing Winning Proposals

Good Grief, Good Grammar

eService Communications

Communicate with Confidence®

Customer Service Communications

Presentations That Work® (oral presentations)

Listening until You Really Hear

Resolving Conflict without Punching Someone Out

Meetings: Leading and Participating

Negotiating So That Everyone Wins

E-mail Excellence™

Managing Information Overload: Increasing Your Personal Productivity

SPEECHES

Communicate with Confidence®: The 10 Cs of Effective Communication

Get a Life without Sacrificing Your Career

The Gender Communication Gap: "Did You Hear What I Think I Said?"

Thinking on Your Feet: Platform Tips for the Presenter

Communicate with Confidence:® From Boardroom to Bedroom

Your Signature Life™

Communicating CARE to Customers

Selling across Gender Lines

Write This Way to Success

Managing Information Overload: Increasing Your Personal Productivity

E-mail Excellence™

Listening until You Really Hear

Leading and Participating in Effective Meetings

Resolving Conflict without Punching Someone Out

Ten Smart Moves for Women

The Worth of a Woman's Words

The Purpose and the Plan—Despite the Pain and the Pace

FOR MORE INFORMATION

Dianna Booher and her staff travel internationally presenting programs on communication and delivering motivational keynote addresses on life balance and personal growth topics. For more information, please contact:

Booher Consultants, Inc.
2051 Hughes Road
Grapevine, TX 76051
Phone: 817-318-6000
mailroom@booher.com
www.booher.com and www.diannabooher.com

ABOUT THE AUTHOR

Dianna Booher is an internationally recognized business communication expert and the author of forty-two books and numerous videos, audios, and Web-based e-learning products for improving communication, sales effectiveness, and productivity. She is the founder and president of Booher Consultants, based in the Dallas–Fort Worth Metroplex. The firm provides communication training (written, oral, interpersonal, gender, customer service) to some of the largest Fortune 500 companies and government agencies, among them: Lockheed Martin, IBM, Kraft, Bank of America, Verizon, J. P. Morgan Chase, Caterpillar, PepsiCo, Frito-Lay, Bayer, Nokia, J. C. Penney, MD Anderson Cancer Center, Morgan Stanley, Ernst & Young, Texas Instruments, the Army and Air Force Exchange Service, Federal Reserve Banks, U.S. Department of Veterans Affairs, and NASA. *Successful Meetings* magazine recognized Dianna in their list of "21 Top Speakers for the 21st Century." Dianna holds a master's degree in English from the University of Houston.

Dianna and her husband, Vernon, also a member of Booher Consultants, have two grown, married children. They live in Texas and are active members of First Church in Euless, Texas.